You don't have to be bored when you diet!

USE THE FINGERTIP
LOW CALORIE GUIDE

CHAPTER 15

to find out which foods are
200-350 calories
100-200 calories
50-100 calories
20-50 calories
20 calories or less

You'll find delicious surprises like these...

Under 20 calories:
1 dill pickle
1 cup spinach

Under 50 calories:
1 egg roll
1 cup popcorn

Under 100 calories:
1 extra light beer
4 ounces gefilte fish

Under 200 calories:
7 ounces beef stew with biscuits
7½ ounces macaroni and cheese

Under 350 calories:
13 ounces eggplant parmigiana
8 ounces oysters

Also by
Bernard Le Gette

*Le Gette's Guide To
Fresh Food Shopping*

Published by
WARNER BOOKS

ATTENTION: SCHOOLS AND CORPORATIONS

WARNER books are available at quantity discounts with bulk purchase for educational, business, or sales promotional use. For information, please write to: SPECIAL SALES DEPARTMENT, WARNER BOOKS, 666 FIFTH AVENUE, NEW YORK, N.Y. 10103.

ARE THERE WARNER BOOKS
YOU WANT BUT CANNOT FIND IN YOUR LOCAL STORES?

You can get any WARNER BOOKS title in print. Simply send title and retail price, plus 50¢ per order and 50¢ per copy to cover mailing and handling costs for each book desired. New York State and California residents add applicable sales tax. Enclose check or money order only, no cash please, to: WARNER BOOKS, P.O. BOX 690, NEW YORK, N.Y. 10019.

LeGette's *Calorie* ENCYCLOPEDIA

Bernard Le Gette

WARNER BOOKS

A Warner Communications Company

WARNER BOOKS EDITION

Copyright © 1983 by Bernard Le Gette
All rights reserved.

Cover photo by Frank Marchesano

Warner Books, Inc.
666 Fifth Avenue
New York, N.Y. 10103

 A Warner Communications Company

Printed in the United States of America

First Printing: January, 1983

15   14   13   12   11

Contents

Contents

Introduction

Losing weight is simple. It's not easy—but it's simple.
You cut the intake of your calories, and then
you lose weight. Everything else you've ever heard
is icing on the cake you can't eat. Carbohydrates,
cholesterol, volume, protein, metabolism, exercise,
are all very interesting, and confusing, to think
about, though none of these things plays a big role
in how much you weigh or how little you can
weigh.

But even when people cut calories they
usually don't do a very good job of it. You have
probably gone on diets, wondered why they
didn't work and wandered off them again, or maybe
they did work, but your will power collapsed—

the constant pressure of not eating so many delicious foods caved you right in.

There are two reasons why most people fail. The first is that they don't really know how many calories they're consuming. They estimate how many calories are in each food, estimate how much of each food they ate, and constantly say things like, "That was only a little snack—two or three crackers." Sound familiar? And of course they're always rejecting potatoes.

Well I'll tell you right now, there is no way you can estimate. You can't estimate the size, you can't estimate the number of calories and you can't estimate the number of times you snacked. You can't estimate a thing. You aren't that smart. Nobody is.

You have to count the pieces, weigh them, and check every time how many calories you just ate. And then you have to write it down. Every calorie. Every day.

Now I know this is more inconvenient than being fat, and hating yourself every day, and being tired, and having heart attacks. But that's the way it is. It does have the advantage of being one inconvenience instead of many, and it is also only one simple way to lose weight—instead of many complicated ways not to—which brings us to the second reason most people fail.

It's because losing weight tends to get very vague in people's minds. It's a hidden enemy

that has to be strained against every day. And that's
very disheartening—which means it won't work.
Any constant general restriction on your life, that
has no definite limits and no clear procedure,
is just not going to work. That's why specific diets
are so successful in the short term—they remove
the vagueness, the guesswork, the doubt. But we
aren't talking about the short term. We're talking
about weighing whatever you like for the rest of
your life.

Fortunately, you don't have to fight hidden
enemies. You don't even have to use much will
power. You only have to know how to count—
calories.

The purpose of this book and the years of
research that went into it is to give you—in
one place—the calories of all the foods you might
ever eat. Whether it's fresh, or a commercially
packaged brand, or a meal you ate in a restaurant
or prepared at home, or a snack you ate at a
drive-in—it's here. The portions listed are as
standardized as is practical, so you don't have
to bring your calculator. There are no extra columns
of things that won't help you lose weight, and
there is as little repetition as possible. You won't find
listings of Thingamajigs—25 calories; Thingamajigs
on a stick—25 calories; Thingamajigs sliced—25
calories, and so on. If thingamajigs are 25 calories,
that's all you need to read—very simple.

The chapters are in a logical order chosen to

help you remember where things are listed. If everything were listed alphabetically you wouldn't know if some fish would be found under fillet, or haddock, or Mrs. Paul's, and even when you found it you couldn't compare it to others of its kind. So everything is in these fourteen basic groupings.

And the fifteenth chapter is the Fingertip Low Calorie Guide. This is an innovation which I hope will enable you to find a variety of low calorie foods at a glance. They are listed in calorie groups so you can plan your shopping, your meals, even your snacks with a specific number of calories in mind. It is also a pretty thorough list of the low calorie foods available. As you'll see in the rest of the book, being called *low calorie* or *dietetic* is no guarantee that a food is low in calories.

Everything is listed for normal usage. That is, if a food is made from a mix, say, the quantity and the calories listed are for the food after it's been prepared according to the package instructions. Likewise, it is of no use to know how many calories are in a pound of spinach while it is still frozen, so that is not listed. Now some things are listed as containing 0 calories for one tsp, and that is accurate; it is also reasonably accurate for one tbs. I can't guarantee, however, that there are no calories in three lbs. of sweetener. There just might be a few.

So how do you lose weight? Eat *what* you want, though of course a balanced diet is always best. It's not what, but *how many* that counts. Remember, virtually all foods have calories. The question is, how much satisfaction and/or nutrition are you getting from a particular food? For the calories in it, a plain potato contains a phenomenal variety of nutrients— you can probably live longer on potatoes than on any other single food—and that would suit some people fine. Others, however, would like to go quickly on apples, which contain neither calories nor nutrients in any marked degree.

But however you do it—eat fewer calories. Measure every portion. It's quite easy. Just put your chicken, or your potato, on a scale, see what the scale says, and compare that to the portion listed in this book. Write down the number of calories for each meal. Add them up at the end of the day, and in the morning write down how much you weigh next to yesterday's calorie total.

But you have to do it every time. It won't do you any good sometimes. And if after awhile you think you can remember most foods' calories, you're wrong. You have to measure. You have to count. The reason you're fat (which is why you bought this book) is you don't know how to play it by eye. You were brought up to eat too much, your aggression makes you hungry, your metabolism is rotten, whatever. It doesn't matter. You want to be thin. I just told you how. If you really *want* to be thin, that's what you'll do. Otherwise you'll continue to play at it and make excuses.

Now if you want to look good and be completely healthy *in addition* to being thin, you'll also exercise, though the exercise won't do either of those things for you if you're overweight. And it won't help you to lose much weight either. The relation between calories and exercise is straightforward. The harder it is, the more calories you burn. There are 3,600 calories in 1 pound of fat. Roughly, you'll burn 100 calories by:

skating (either kind)	45	minutes
skiing (either kind)	35	"
football	30	"
handball	22	"
walking	19	"
rowing	18	"
bicycling	15	"
chopping wood	13	"
swimming	12	"
jumping rope	11	"
jogging	10	"
running	6	"

or (even more roughly) 18 holes of golf (on foot) or two sets of tennis.

So if you want to lose that pound of fat, it's easier not to eat the 3,600 calories than to jump rope for 7 hours. What will help the most is a regular, steady approach to food and calories. This book can be your guide to help you look and feel the person you really want to be.

1 quart	=	4 cups
1 cup	=	8 fluid ounces (oz)
1 cup	=	½ pint
1 cup	=	16 tablespoons
1 ounce	=	2 tablespoons
1 tablespoon (tbs.)	=	3 teaspoons
1 jigger, or shot	=	1½ ounces
1 pound (lb.)	=	16 ounces

Remember, a fluid ounce is a measure of volume, not weight.

ALL listings are for food *as prepared* for normal usage. That means that after it's been prepared with all the normal ingredients, and it's ready to eat—that's what the calories are for.

CHAPTER 1

Beverages

SPIRITS, WINES, LIQUEURS, COCKTAILS, BRANDIES, AND COCKTAIL MIXES

Note: The number of calories in distilled spirits depends entirely on the alcoholic content—the higher the proof, the higher the calories. This is true for bourbon, gin, rum, Scotch, tequila, vodka, and almost anything called whiskey.

1

Distilled Spirits, 1 oz

80 proof	65
90 proof	75
100 proof	85
150 proof	125

Cocktails, canned or bottled, alcoholic, 1 oz

Amaretto Sour
  Mr. Boston — 40
Apricot Sour
  Party Tyme — 33
Banana Daiquiri
  Party Tyme — 33
Daiquiri
  Hiram Walker — 59
  Mr. Boston — 33
  Party Tyme — 33
  Calvert — 63
Gimlet
  Party Tyme — 40
Gin & Tonic
  Party Tyme — 28
Mai Tai
  Lemon Hart — 60
  Mr. Boston — 36
  Party Tyme — 33

Sour, Gin
  Calvert — 65
Sour, Scotch
  Party Tyme — 33
Sour, Tequila
  Calvert — 65
Sour, Whiskey
  Calvert — 60
  Hiram Walker — 60
  Mr. Boston — 40
Tequila Sunrise
  Mr. Boston — 40
Tom Collins
  Calvert — 65
  Party Tyme — 29
Vodka Tonic
  Party Tyme — 27
Wallbanger
  Mr. Boston — 34

Cocktail Mixes, bottled and dry, nonalcoholic, 1 oz or 1 premeasured packet

Alexander
  Holland House — 69
Amaretto
  Holland House — 79
Banana Daiquiri
  Holland House — 66

Black Russian
Holland House   92

Bloody Mary
Holland House   6
Party Tyme   29

Coconut
Holland House   117

Daiquiri
Holland House   46
Party Tyme   35
Party Tyme instant   56

Gimlet
Holland House   24
Party Tyme instant   41

Grasshopper
Holland House   69

Mai Tai
Holland House   26
Party Tyme   24
Party Tyme instant   53

Manhattan
Holland House   29

Margarita
Holland House   39
Party Tyme   23
Party Tyme instant   35

Martini
Holland House   10
Party Tyme   17

1

Mint Julep
Holland House   67

Old Fashioned
Holland House   9
Party Tyme   28

Piña Colada
Holland House   60
Party Tyme   50

Pink Squirrel
Holland House   69

Planter's Punch
Party Tyme   37

Screwdriver
Holland House   69
Party Tyme   21

Sidecar
Holland House   17

Sour, Blackberry
Holland House   50

Sour, Virgin
Party Tyme   50

Sour, Whiskey
Canada Dry   11
Holland House   53
Holland House low calorie   9
Party Tyme   29
Party Tyme instant   53

Sip 'n Slim
Holland House   10

Strawberry Sting
  Holland House   35
Tom Collins
  Holland House   58
  Party Tyme   44
  Party Tyme instant   58

Cocktails, standard recipe, alcoholic, 1 oz alcohol, unless noted

Bacardi   155
Bloody Mary   140
Brandy Alexander   225
Bourbon Highball (1½ oz bourbon)
  with soda   125
  with ginger ale   180
Cuba Libre   224
Daiquiri   135
Gimlet   136
Gin Fizz   172
Grasshopper   235
Irish Coffee   214
Manhattan   177
Martini, Gin or Vodka   115
Mint Julep   209
Old Fashioned   144
Orange Blossom   153
Pink Lady   190
Rob Roy   199

1

Rum Cola (see Cuba Libre)	224
Screwdriver	168
Side Car	161
Sloe Gin Fizz	155
Stinger	149
Tom Collins	170
Whiskey Sour	142

Wines, 4 oz

Alsatian	
Wilm	88
Altar, red	
Gold Seal	132
Henri Marchant	132
Blackberry	
Manischewitz	180
Bordeaux	
red	
B&G Margaux	83
B&G Prince Noir	81
B&G Saint-Emilion	84
Chanson	108
Cruse	92
Cruse Saint-Emilion	92
Cruse Saint-Julien	92
Cruse Médoc	96
Cruse Château La Garde	108

1

Gold Seal blanc de blancs 98
   brut 81
   dry 91
Great Western brut 100
   dry 104
   pink 108
Henri Marchant blanc de blancs 88
   brut 91
   dry 98
Lejon 94
Korbel 104
Manischewitz 88
Mumm's brut 88
   dry 111
Taylor brut 101
   dry 104
   pink 108
Veuve Clicquot 104

Chianti
Brolio 88
Gancia 88
Italian Swiss Colony 87

Claret
Gold Seal 109
Inglenook 80
Italian Swiss Colony 86
Louis Martini 126
Taylor 96

Cold Duck
Gold Seal 97

Great Western	121
Taylor	120
Concord	
Gold Seal	132
Henri Marchant	132
Manischewitz	
red	160
white	130
medium dry	120
dry	85
Mogen David	160
Kosher	
Manischewitz	
sweet	170
medium	112
dry	91
Labrusca	
Gold Seal	130
Henri Marchant	132
Lake Country	
Taylor	106
Liebfraumilch	
Anheuser & Fehrs	80
Dienhard	95
Malaga	
Manischewitz	180
Moselle	
Dienhard	95
Julius Kayser	77

B&G	93
Riesling	
Dienhard	96
Gold Seal	92
Henri Marchant	92
Inglenook	82
Louis Martini	120
Rosé	
Cruse	96
Gold Seal	99
Henri Marchant	96
Italian Swiss Colony	86
Taylor	92
Sake	151
Sancerre	
B&G	80
Sauterne	
Gallo	67
Gallo Haut	83
Gold Seal	97
Gold Seal Haut	109
Great Western	105
Henri Marchant	109
Italian Swiss Colony	77
Louis Martini	120
Mogen David cream	59
Mogen David dry	39
Taylor	105
Soave	
Antinori	110

Thunderbird
   Gallo   139
Valpolicella
   Antinori   109
Zinfandel
   Inglenook   76
   Italian Swiss Colony   80
   Louis Martini   120

Aperitif and Dessert Wines, 4 oz

Asti Spumante
   Gancia   168
Aquavit
   Leroux   300
Campari   66
   Dubonnet Blonde   151
   Dubonnet Red   190
Madeira
   Gold Seal   144
   Henri Marchant   144
   Leacock   160
   Sandeman   168
Muscatel
   Gallo   144
   Gold Seal   210
Pernod
   Julius Wyle   315

1

Port

Gallo	146
Gold Seal	185
Great Western	178
Italian Swiss Colony	170
Louis Martini	215
Robertson	180
Sandeman	184
Taylor	195

Sherry

Gallo	104
Gold Seal	185
Great Western	156
Taylor	200
Dry Sack	160

Sherry, cream

Gallo	150
Gold Seal	205
Great Western	180
Louis Martini	175
Taylor	178

Sherry, dry

Gallo	110
Gold Seal	162
Great Western	140
Italian Swiss Colony	132
Louis Martini	180
Sandeman	145
Taylor	152

Vermouth, dry
    C&P   148
    Gallo   100
    Gancia   168
    Great Western   113
    Lejon   129
    Noilly Pratt   136
    Taylor   136

Vermouth, sweet
    C&P   156
    Gallo   150
    Gancia   185
    Great Western   172
    Lejon   174
    Noilly Pratt   172
    Taylor   175

Cordials and Liqueurs, 1 oz

Amaretto   80
Anise   82
Anisette
    Bols   111
    DuBouchett   85
    DeKuyper   95
    Garnier   82
    Mr. Boston   90
    Mr. Boston Connoisseur   64

Apricot
Bols	96
Dolfi	100
DuBouchett	65

B & B	94
Benai	110
Benedictine	110

Blackberry
Bols	90
Dolfi	89
DuBouchett	68

Brandy, flavored
Bols	100
DuBouchett	87
Garnier	6
Leroux	90
Mr. Boston	100
Mr. Boston Connoisseur	75

Cherry liqueur
Bols	96
DeKuyper	75
Dolfi	87
DuBouchett	72
Hiram Walker	82
Leroux	82

Chocolate
Vandermint	90

Claristine
Leroux	114

Coffee
Tia Maria   92
Pasha   100
Crème de almond
DuBouchett   100
Crème de apricot
Mr. Boston   90
Mr. Boston Connoisseur   65
Crème de banana
Garnier   90
Mr. Boston   90
Mr. Boston Connoisseur   65
Crème de cacao
Bols   100
Dolfi   100
DuBouchett   100
Garnier   100
Hiram Walker   100
Mr. Boston   90
Mr. Boston Connoisseur   65
Crème de cassis
Leroux   87
Mr. Boston   90
Crème de menthe   100
Crème de noisette   90
Crème de noyaux
Bols   115
Mr. Boston   99
Crème de peach
Mr. Boston Connoisseur   65

Curaçao 100
Drambuie 110
Grenadine 81
Kirsch 80
Kümmel
  DuBouchett
    48 proof 65
    70 proof 83
  Garnier 75
  Hiram Walker 71
  Leroux 75
  Mr. Boston 78
Lochon Ora
  Leroux 89
Peach Liqueur
  Bols 96
  DeKuyper 82
  Dolfi 103
  DuBouchett 67
  Hiram Walker 81
  Leroux 85
Raspberry Liqueur
  Dolfi 80
  DuBouchett 56
Rock & Rye
  DuBouchett
    60 proof 78
    70 proof 86
  Garnier 83
  Mr. Boston 90

Mr. Boston Connoisseur	65

Schnapps, peppermint

DuBouchett	85
Garnier	83
Hiram Walker	78
Leroux	87
Mr. Boston	77

Sloe Gin

Bols	85
DeKuyper	70
Dolfi	114
DuBouchett	70
Garnier	83
Mr. Boston	67

Triple Sec

Bols	104
Dolfi	107
DuBouchett	61
Garnier	83
Hiram Walker	105
Leroux	104
Mr. Boston	100

BEER, ALE, MALT LIQUOR,
12 oz

Andeker	160
Black Horse Ale	162
Brauhaus	150

1

Buckeye	144
Budweiser	156
Budweiser Malt Liquor	160
Busch Bavarian	155
Carling Black Label	160
Carlsberg Light	159
Carlsberg Dark	240
Champale Malt Liquor	157
Country Club Malt Liquor	163
Coors	138
Eastside Lager	145
Falstaff	150
Gablinger's	99
Goebel	145
Grand Union	150
Grenzquell	150
Hamms	138
Heidelberg	133
Heidelberg Light	129
Heileman's	158
Kingsbury	146
Knickerbocker	160
Meister Brau	144
Meister Brau Draft	144
Meister Brau Lite	96
Michelob	160
Michelob Light	134
Miller	150
Miller Lite	96
Natural Light	110

Old Dutch	150
Old Milwaukee	144
Old Ranger	150
Pabst Blue Ribbon	150
Pabst Light	100
Pabst Extra Light	70
Pearl	145
Pilser's	152
Red Cap Ale	159
Rheingold	160
Schaefer	158
Schlitz	148
Schlitz Light	96
Schmidt's	142
Stag	151
Stroh Bohemian	136
Stroh Bock	155
Stroh Light	115
Tuborg USA	140
Tudor	150

Near Beer, 12 oz

Goetz Pale	78
Kingsbury	45

1

Nonalcoholic Beer, 12 oz

Maltcrest	70
Metbrew	70
Zing	65

SOFT DRINKS, 8 oz

Note: Virtually all sodas that are called *low calorie*, *sugar free*, or *dietetic* contain 2 calories or less.

Aspen	105
Birch Beer	
Canada Dry	110
Pennsylvania Dutch	109
Yukon Club	116
Bitter lemon	
Canada Dry	104
Schweppes	128
Bitter orange	
Schweppes	124
Bubble Up	97
Cactus Cooler	120
Cherry	
Cott	123
Crush	121

Fanta	117
Mission	122
Club soda, all brands	0
Coconut	
Yoo-Hoo	117
Coffee	
Hoffman	88
Cola	
Canada Dry	110
Coca-Cola	96
Pepsi-Cola	104
Royal Crown	109
Pepsi Light	47
Shasta	90
Cream	
Canada Dry	127
Fanta	130
Shasta	90
Schweppes	115
Dr. Brown's Cel-Ray Tonic	89
Dr. Nehi	98
Dr. Pepper	98
Fruit punch	
Shasta	110
Fruit mix	
Wyler's	88
Ginger Ale	
Canada Dry	85
Fanta	85
Nehi	91

Schweppes	88
Ginger Beer	
Schweppes	96
Grape	
Canada Dry	130
Crush	120
Fanta	114
Nehi	116
Patio	128
Schweppes	129
Shasta	114
Grapefruit	
Fanta	115
Shasta	103
Half and Half	110
Hi Spot	100
Kick	118
Kool Aid, all flavors	93
Lemon	
Hi-C	123
Shasta	97
Lemon-Lime	
Shasta	93
Lime	
Canada Dry	130
Mello-Yello	115
Mr. PiBB	93
Mountain Dew	118
Orange	
Canada Dry	130

Crush 120
Fanta 114
Hi-C 101
Nedick's 121
Nehi 124
Patio 128
Schweppes 118
Shasta 114
Sunkist 125

Pineapple
Canada Dry 110

Purple Passion
Canada Dry 120

Quinine Water
Canada Dry 95
Fanta 84
Schweppes 88

Rondo
Schweppes 100

Root Beer
A&W 114
Berks County 116
Canada Dry Barrelhead 110
Canada Dry Rooti 110
Dad's 105
Fanta 103
Hires 100
On Tap 105
Patio 110
Royal Crown 113

Schweppes	105
Shasta	100
7-Up	97
Sprite	95
Squirt	91
Strawberry	
Canada Dry	120
Crush	121
Fanta	121
Nehi	116
Shasta	94
Yoo-Hoo	124
Sun-Drop	118
Teem	93
Tahitian Treat	
Canada Dry	130
Tiki	100
Tonic	
Canada Dry	90
Schweppes	88
Shasta	66
Upper 10	101
Vanilla	
Yoo-Hoo	125
Vanilla Cream	
Canada Dry	130
Wild Cherry	
Canada Dry	130
Wink	120

COFFEE AND TEA, 6 oz

1

Coffee
regular	2
instant	4
flavored	
General Foods	
Cafe Francais	60
Cafe Vienna	60
Orange Cappuccino	60
Suisse Mocha	60
Postum	10
Tea, bags or loose	1
Tea, bottled or canned	
Lipton	84
sugar free	1
No-Cal	0
Tea, instant	
Lipton lemon-flavored	3
100% Tea	0
Nestea	1
Tender Leaf	1
Tea, mix, iced, lemon-flavored	
Our Own (A&P)	62
Lipton	40
Nestea	15
with sugar	70

1

Salada	57
Wyler's	56

FRUIT AND VEGETABLE
JUICES, 6 oz

Fresh

Grapefruit	70
Lemon or Lime	45
Lemon or Lime, 1 Tbsp	3
Orange	
California	85
Florida	80
Valencia	85
Peach Nectar	90
Tangerine	80

Bottled and Canned

Apple	
Ann Page	90
Heinz	75

Musselman's	80
Mott's	80
Pillsbury	60
Seneca	80
Welch's	90
Apple-Cranberry	
Lincoln	104
Apricot nectar	
Del Monte	100
Heart's Delight	194
Heinz	104
Libby's	110
Seneca	75
Cranberry-Apple	
Cranapple	120
Fig	
Real Fig	135
Fig and Prune	
Fig 'n' Prune	135
Grape	
Heinz	120
Seneca	110
Welch's	120
Grapefruit	
Del Monte	70
Heinz	70
Libby's	75
Ocean Spray	70
Seneca	55
Stokely-Van Camp	60

Welch's	75
Grapefruit-Orange	
Seneca	77
Grenadine syrup, nonalcoholic, 1 oz.	
Garnier	100
Giroux	104
Lemon, 1 Tbsp	
ReaLemon	4
Rose's	5
Lime, 1 Tbsp	
ReaLime	6
Orange	
Del Monte	80
Heinz	75
Libby's	90
Welch's	90
Orange-Grapefruit	
Del Monte	80
Libby's	80
Stokely-Van Camp	70
Peach Nectar	
Del Monte	100
Libby's	90
Heart's Delight	89
Pear Nectar	
Del Monte	110
Libby's	100
Heart's Delight	95
Pineapple	
Del Monte	100

Dole	93
Heinz	95
Seneca	68
Stokely-Van Camp	110
Pineapple-Grapefruit	
Del Monte	90
Pineapple-Orange	
Ann Page	87
Del Monte	90
Hi-C	94
Lincoln	97
Prune	
Ann Page	140
Del Monte	120
Heinz	130
Mott's	140
RealPrune	130
Seneca	130
Sunsweet	124
Welch's	150
Tomato	
Campbell's	35
Del Monte	35
Heinz	38
Hunt's	43
Libby's	39
Sacramento	32
Seneca	27
Stokely-Van Camp	33
Townhouse	35

Welch's	38
Vegetable	
Campbell V-8	35
Vegemato	32

Frozen Juice

Grape
Minute Maid	99
Snow Crop	99

Grapefruit
Bird's Eye	68
Minute Maid	75
Snow Crop	75

Lemon
Minute Maid	40

Orange
Bright and Early	90
Minute Maid	90
Snow Crop	120
Stokely-Van Camp	90

Orange-Grapefruit
Bird's Eye	72
Minute Maid	76

Pineapple
Dole	101
Minute Maid	92

Pineapple-orange
   Minute Maid   94
   Dole   77
Tangerine
   Minute Maid   86
   Snow Crop   85

Dairy-Packed Juice, 8 oz

Grapefruit
   Tropicana   75
Orange
   Borden   96
   Kraft   90
   Sealtest   96
   Tropicana   83
Orange-Grapefruit
   Kraft   90
Orange-Pineapple
   Ann Page   87
   Hi-C   94
   Kraft   96

FRUIT-FLAVORED DRINKS, ALL TYPES, 6 oz

Apple
Ann Page	90
Hi-C	90

Apple-Grape
Mott's	90
Welch's	92

Apricot-Apple
BC	92

Cherry
Ann Page	90
Hi-C	75

Citrus Cooler
Ann Page	90
Hi-C	90

Cranberry
Ann Page	120
Ocean Spray	105
Seneca	120
Welch's	105

Cranberry-Apple
Ann Page	135
Lincoln	103
Mott's	95
Ocean Spray	135

Cranberry-Apricot
Ocean Spray   105
Cranberry-Grape
Ocean Spray   105
Welch's   120
Cranberry-Orange
Knox   59
Cranberry-Prune
Ocean Spray   120
Grape
Ann Page   90
Hi-C   90
Welch's   90
Grape-Apple
BC   107
Grapefruit
Ann Page   80
Sealtest   90
Tropicana   70
Lemon
Sealtest   90
Lemonade
Bird's Eye   74
Borden   78
Country Time   67
Hi-C   75
Minute Maid   75
RealLemon   76
Sealtest   80
Snow Crop   75

Stokely-Van Camp	80
Wyler's	67
Lemon-Limeade	
Minute Maid	75
Snow Crop	75
Limeade	
Bird's Eye	75
Minute Maid	75
Snow Crop	75
Orange	
A&P	80
Ann Page	90
Bird's Eye	105
Borden	85
Hi-C	125
Minute Maid	125
Start	120
Stokely-Van Camp	114
Tang	120
Tropicana	93
Welch's	135
Orange-Pineapple	
Ann Page	120
BC	120
Start	120
Peach	
Hi-C	120
Pineapple-Grapefruit	
Dole	120

Punch
Ann Page — 120
Hawaiian Punch — 120
Hi-C — 130
Mott's — 120
Stokely-Van Camp — 114
Tropicana — 93
Welch's — 130
Wyler's — 85

Raspberry
Wyler's — 85

Strawberry
Hi-C — 120
Wyler's — 85

Tangerine
Hi-C — 120

Wild Berry
Ann Page — 120
Hi-C — 115

CHAPTER 2

Dairy

BUTTER AND MARGARINE

Butter
  ½ cup (¼ lb)   815
  1 Tbsp   100
Butter, whipped
  ½ cup   540
  1 Tbsp   65
Margarine, 1 Tbsp
  Imitation
    Mazola   50
    Parkay   50
    Weight Watchers   50

Regular and Soft, all brands	100
Diet, all brands	50
Spread	
Blue Bonnet	80
Fleishmann	80
Parkay	70
Whipped, all brands	70

CHEESE, 1 oz unless noted

American	
Borden	104
Kraft	90
Blue	
Borden	105
Casino	100
Kraft	99
Brie	
Dorman	100
Kraft	100
Camembert	
Borden	85
Kraft	85
Caraway	
Kraft	111
Cheddar	
Borden	113
Kraft	113

Colby
  Borden   111
  Kraft   111

Cottage, 1 cup
  creamed
  Borden   240
  Breakstone   230
  Breakstone low-fat   180
  Foremost   212
  Friendship   360
  Kraft   214
  Lucerne   240
  Meadow Gold   134
  Sealtest   114

  partly creamed
  Meadow Gold   204
  Sealtest   176

  uncreamed, potstyle
  Borden   196
  Breakstone   170
  Kraft   206
  Sealtest   180

  low fat
  Borden   180
  Breakstone   180
  Friendship   200
  Lucerne   200
  Viva   200
  Weight Watchers   180

Cream cheese
    Borden   96
    Kraft Philadelphia Brand   98

Edam
    Dorman   105
    House of Gold   105

Farmer's
    Breakstone   30
    Dutch Garden   100
    Friendship   38
    Wispride   100

Fondue
    Swiss Knight   60

Fontina
    Kraft   114

Frankenmuth
    Kraft   113

Gjetost
    Kraft   135

Gorgonzola
    Kraft   112

Gouda
    Borden   86
    Kraft   108

Gruyère
    Borden   101
    Kraft   108
    Swiss Knight   101

Leyden
    Kraft   80

Liederkranz
  Borden   86
Limburger
  Borden   97
  Dorman   100
  Kraft   98
  Mountain Valley   100
Monterey Jack
  Borden   103
  Casino   100
  Kraft   103
Mozzarella
  Borden   79
  Kraft   79
  Dorman   85
Muenster
  Borden   85
  Dorman   90
  Kraft   100
Neufchâtel
  Borden   73
  Kraft   69
Nuworld
  Kraft   104
Parmesan, grated, 1 Tbsp
  Buitoni   23
  Kraft   27
  La Rosa   33
  Lucerne   25

Parmesan & Romano, grated, 1 Tbsp
   Borden   30
   Kraft   30

Pimiento
   Borden   104
   Kraft   104

Port Salut
   Dorman   100
   Kraft   100

Premost
   Kraft   134

Provolone
   Borden   93
   Kraft   99

Ricotta
   Borden   42
   Kraft   99

Romano, grated, 1 Tbsp
   Buitoni   21
   Kraft   26

Roquefort
   Borden   107
   Kraft   105

Sap Sago
   Kraft   76

Sardo Romano
   Kraft   110

Scamorze
   Kraft   100

Swiss
  Borden   104
  Dorman   90
  Kraft   104
Sage
  Kraft   113
Tilsit
  Dorman   95

Cheese Food

American
  Borden   92
  Kraft   77
Blue
  Borden   82
  Borden Vera Blue   91
  Wispride   100
Cheddar
  Wispride   100
Jalapeno pepper
  Kraft   93
Munst-ett
  Kraft   101
Pimiento
  Borden   91
  Pauley Swiss   90
  Velveeta   90
Pizza
  Kraft   80

Sharp
   Kraft   93
Swiss
   Borden   91
   Kraft   91

Cheese Spread

American
   Borden   85
   Kraft   77
   Kraft Old English   97
American with Bacon
   Borden   80
   Kraft   92
Blue
   Borden   82
   Roka   80
   Wispride   92
Cheddar
   Snack Mate   85
   Wispride   97
Garlic
   Borden   82
   Kraft   86
Limburger
   Borden   82

Mohawk Valley	70
Moose	70
Pimiento	
Cheez Whiz	76
Kraft	77
Snack Mate	90
Smoked	
Borden	80
Velveeta	80

CREAM, 1 Tbsp

half and half	
Borden	19
Meadow Gold	27
Sealtest	20
light	
Borden	25
Foremost	30
Sealtest	35
medium	
Borden	41
Sealtest	42
heavy (whipping)	
Borden	52

Foremost	52
Lucerne	10
Sealtest	52

Sour Cream, 1 Tbsp

Borden	29
Borden half and half	29
Borden imitation	25
Foremost	30
Sealtest	29

Non-Dairy Creamers, 1 Tsp

coffee creamers
Carnation Coffee-Mate	11
Meadow Gold	9
Pet Cremora	11

whipped toppings
Reddi-Whip	7
Sta-Whip	8

EGGS

Chicken

  raw, boiled, or poached

    medium   72

    large   82

    extra large   94

  raw, white only

    medium   15

    large   18

    extra large   20

    1 cup   125

  raw, yolk only

    medium   53

    large   60

    extra large   68

  fried

    medium   85

    large   97

    extra large   113

  scrambled or omelet

    medium   99

    large   110

    extra large   127

Duck, raw   130

Goose, raw   266

Turkey, raw   135

Egg Mixes, Commercial

Imitation
Morningstar Farms Scramblers, ½ cup	130
Tillie Lewis Eggstra, 1 pkt	101
Fleishmann Egg Beaters, ½ cup	81

Omelets, 1 pkt
Plain
Durkee	604
Durkee dry mix	112

with bacon
Durkee	620
Durkee dry mix	125

with cheese
Durkee	617
Durkee dry mix	127
McCormick	130
Schilling	128

Western
Durkee	604
Durkee dry mix	112
McCormick	115
Schilling	115

Scrambled
Durkee	124

with bacon
Durkee	180

with sausage and potatoes
Swanson	452

MILK, 8 oz

Buttermilk
Borden
  .1% fat   88
  .5% fat   90
  1% fat   107
  1.5% fat   110
  2% fat   122
  3% fat   158
Friendship 1.4% fat   120
Golden Nugget .8%   92
Light 'n Lively .8% fat   95
Lucerne 1.5% fat   120
Sealtest 2% fat   114

Skim
Borden .1% fat   81
Lucerne
  0% fat   90
  1% fat   110
  2% fat   130
Meadow Gold
  .5% fat   87
  2% fat   130
Sealtest .1% fat   79

Skim Fortified
Borden   81
Borden Lite Line   117
Borden Hi Protein   132

Gail Borden	81
Light 'n Lively	114
Sealtest	137
Whole	
Borden	160
Foremost	154
Lucerne	160
Meadow Gold	166
Sealtest	150
Whole Fortified	
Gail Borden	159
Sealtest Multivitamin	151

Milk Beverages, 8 oz unless noted

Cherry-vanilla	
Borden	291
Chocolate	
Borden	210
Meadow Gold	190
Sealtest	175
Chocolate fudge	
Borden	284
Chocolate mixes	
Carnation Instant, 1 pkt	130
Carnation Slender, 1 pkt	110
Nestle's Quik	215

Ovaltine, 1 oz	105
Pillsbury, 1 pkt	295
Safeway, 2 tsp	215
Sealtest	195
Chocolate malt mix	
Carnation Instant, 1 pkt	130
Carnation Slender, 1 pkt	110
Eggnog, dairy packed	
Borden	
4.7% fat	260
6% fat	302
8% fat	375
Carnation, 1 pkt	130
Meadow Gold	327
Sealtest	324
Malt	
Borden	80
Carnation	90
Ovaltine	100
Mocha	
Borden	291
Strawberry	
Borden	287
Carnation, 1 pkt	130
Pillsbury, 1 pkt	290
Vanilla	
Borden	291
Carnation, 1 pkt	130

YOGURT, 8 oz

Plain

Borden Lite-Line	140
Borden Swiss Style	167
Breakstone	144
Dannon	150
Light 'n Lively	140
Lucerne	160
Pet	157
Viva	180

Flavored, all flavors

Borden	270
Breyer's	270
Dannon	210
Light 'n Lively	240
Meadow Gold	270
Viva	250

Frozen

Danny

In-A-Cup, 8 oz.	180
On-A-Stick, uncoated	65

CHAPTER 3

Breads, Crackers, Flour

BREAD, 1 slice, approximately 1 oz unless noted

Tasty Bake	70
Date Nut	
Thomas	100
French	
Pepperidge Farm	79
Wonder	75
Garlic	
Stouffer	80
Gluten	
Thomas	32
Hollywood	70
Honey Bran	
Pepperidge Farm	58
Honey Wheatberry	
Arnold	90
Pepperidge Farm	60
Italian	
Pepperidge Farm	81
Naturel	
Arnold	65
Nut	
Brownberry	85
Oatmeal	
Brownberry	82
Pepperidge Farm	66
Profile	52
Protein	
Thomas	45
Pumpernickel	
Arnold	75

Pepperidge Farm   79

Raisin

  Plain

    Arnold   75

    Thomas   66

  with cinnamon

    Brownberry   85

    Pepperidge Farm   75

    Thomas   65

  with nuts

    Brownberry   95

Rice Cakes

  Spiral   36

Rye

  Arnold   50

    Jewish   75

    soft   75

  Brownberry   65

  Pepperidge Farm   82

  Tasty Bake   91

  Wonder   75

Sourdough

  Di Carlo   71

Wheat

  Arnold

    Granary   71

    Branola   90

    Brick Oven   60

    Melba Thin   40

  Brownberry   85

Buckwheat	75
Colonial	72
Home Pride	75
Pepperidge Farm	70
Pepperidge Farm Very Thin	40
Thomas	50
Wonder	75

Wheat Germ

Pepperidge Farm	69

White

Arnold

Brick Oven, .8 oz slice	65
Brick Oven, 1.1 oz slice	85
Country	95
Hearthstone Country	70
Melba Thin	40
Brownberry Sandwich	75
Brownberry Thin	70
Butternut	75
Colonial	75
Daffodil Farm	58
Fresh Horizons	50
Hart	75
Heartstone	85
Home Pride	75
Homestyle	75
Manor	75
Pepperidge Farm	75
Pepperidge Farm Sandwich	72
Sweetheart	75

Tasty Bake	72
Thomas	64
Weight Watchers	35
Wonder	75
Whole Wheat	
Pepperidge Farm	61
Thomas	65

Bread, Canned, ½ inch slice

Banana Nut	
Dromedary	71
Brown	
B&M	52
Chocolate Nut	
Cross & Blackwell	65
Dromedary	87
Date Nut	
Dromedary	75
Fruit and Nut	
Cross & Blackwell	77
Orange Nut	
Cross & Blackwell	76
Dromedary	78
Spice Nut	
Cross & Blackwell	65

Bread Mixes

White, ¼ loaf
  Pillsbury   460
Cornbread, 1 pkg
  Pillsbury   320
  Aunt Jemima   330

BISCUITS, MUFFINS AND ROLLS

Biscuits, Baking Powder, 1 biscuit

  1869 Brand   105
   prebaked   100
  Pillsbury   70
  Tenderflake   60

Biscuits, refrigerated, 1 biscuit

Plain
  Ballard   50
  Borden   59
  Hungry Jack   95
   Flaky   90

Pillsbury	55
Flaky Baking Powder	67
Tenderflake	
Baking Powder	60
Buttermilk	
Hungry Jack	
Extra Rich	65
Flaky	80
Fluffy	100
Pillsbury	50
Big Country	95
Extra Light	55
Tenderflake	55
Corn Bread	
Pillsbury	95

Muffins, frozen, 1 muffin

Blueberry	
Thomas	110
Howard Johnson	121
Morton	120
Rounds	110
Pepperidge Farm	130
Corn	
Howard Johnson	118
Morton	
regular	130

Rounds	125
Pepperidge Farm	140
Thomas	120
English	
Thomas	130
Orange	
Howard Johnson	115
Raisin Bran	
Pepperidge Farm	130

Muffins, Mix, 1 muffin

Apple Cinnamon	
Betty Crocker	160
Banana Nut	
Betty Crocker	185
Blueberry	
Betty Crocker	120
Corn	
Betty Crocker	160
Orange	
Betty Crocker	155
Pineapple	
Betty Crocker	125

Muffins, packaged

Bran
  Thomas 118
Cinnamon Raisin
  Pepperidge Farm 140
Corn
  Thomas 180
  Toast-r-Cakes 120
English
  Di Carlo 145
  Hostess 145
  Thomas 140
  Wonder 144
Honey Butter
  Arnold Orowheat 150
Onion
  Thomas 130
Raisin
  Wonder 155
Sourdough
  Wonder 130
Wheat
  Home Pride 140

3

Muffins, refrigerated, 1 muffin

Apple Cinnamon
  Pillsbury   155
Corn
  Pillsbury   130

Rolls, 1 roll

Hard Rolls
  Pepperidge Farm   120
    French, 3 oz   264
    French, 5 oz   395
    Hearth   64
    Sesame Crisp   76
  Wonder   82
Sandwich and Hamburger Rolls
  Arnold
    Dutch Egg Buns   130
    Francisco   180
    Soft   110
    Hamburger   110
    Hot Dog   110
  Colonial   160
  Pepperidge Farm   120
  Wonder   160
Soft Rolls
  Arnold

Deli-Twist	110
Finger, 24's and 12's	55
Francisco	100
Refrigerator	95
Ballard	95
Borden	
Gem Flake	70
Onion	95
Colonial	80
Home Pride	90
Pepperidge Farm	
Butter Crescent	130
Dinner	65
Finger	60
Golden Twist	120
Old Fashioned	37
Parkerhouse	60
Party	35
Pillsbury	
Butterflake	110
Crescent	95
Hot Roll Mix	95
Wonder	
Buttermilk	85
Pan	105
Sweet Rolls, refrigerated	
Caramel	
Pillsbury	160
Cinnamon	
Ballard	100

Hungry Jack	145
Pillsbury	114
Orange	
Pillsbury	130
Scones	
Hostess	188

CRACKERS, 1 piece

Bacon Flavored

Keebler	15
Nabisco Bacon Thins	11

Barbecue

Chit Chat	14
Sunshine	17

Butter

Hi-Ho	17
Keebler	
Butter Thins	17
Club	15
Townhouse	19
Nabisco	15
Ritz	17
Tam-Tams	13

Butter-cheese

Ritz	18

Caraway
   Caraway Crazy — 15

Cheese
   Cheese-Nips — 5
   Cheese Tid-Bits — 4
   Cheez-It — 6
   Che-Zo — 5
   Keebler — 11
   Pepperidge Farm — 12

Cheese-peanut Butter
   Keebler — 14

Chicken
   Chicken In a Biskit — 10

Club
   Keebler — 15

Flings Curls
   Nabisco — 10

Gold Fish
   Pepperidge Farm, 1 oz — 140

Ham
   Nabisco — 12

Hi-Ho
   Sunshine — 18

Kavli Flatbread — 35

Matzos
   Goodman's Square — 110
   Goodman's Tea — 75
   Horowitz-Margareten — 130
   Manischewitz
      Egg — 132

Nabisco
   Premium   12
   Royal Lunch   54
   Uneeda   22
Sunshine   11

Sesame
Keebler   16
Meal Mates   22
Sesame Sillys   15
Sunshine   24

Shapies   10

Sip'N Chips   10

Sociables
Nabisco   10

Toasts
Dutch Rusk   60
Holland Rusk   39
Keebler   15
Old London   11
Pepperidge Farm   11
Sunshine All-Rye   21

Soda and water crackers
Huntley & Palmer   35
Jacob's Golden Puffs   34
Keebler Milk Lunch   27
Waldorf   18
Zesta   14

Tomato-onion
Sunshine   15

Town House
Keebler   15
Triangle Thins
Nabisco   8
Twig⁀
Nabisco   14
Waffle crackers   22
Waverly wafers
Nabisco   18
Wheat
Nabisco
   Wheat Toast   15
   Wheat Thins   9
Zwieback
Nabisco   31

OTHER BREAD PRODUCTS

Breadcrumbs, 1 cup   450

Contadina   450
4C plain   410
4C seasoned   400

Breadsticks, 1 piece

onion
  Stella D'Oro   35
plain
  Stella D'Oro   40
sesame
  Stella D'Oro   38
dietetic
  Stella D'Oro   43

Croutons, ½ cup unless noted

bacon
  Bel Air   80
  Brownberry   90
cheese and garlic
  Bel Air   100
garlic
  Bel Air   80
Italian cheese
  Bel Air   100
plain
  Bel Air   60
seasoned
  Bel Air   90
  Brownberry   90

Stuffing, mixes, 1 pkg

Pepperidge Farm	110
Stove Top	170
Uncle Ben's	120

FLOURS, 1 cup

Buckwheat	
dark	325
light	340
Cake	370
Carob	250
Corn	485
Corn Starch, 1 Tbsp	35
Lima Bean	430
Peanut	225
Rye	
light	315
medium	310
dark	420
Soybean, defatted	325
full fat	300
low fat	310
Tortilla	
corn	410

wheat	450
Wheat, all purpose	485
bread	500
cake	430
gluten	530
self-rising	440
whole wheat	400
White	400
Unbleached	400

Meal, 1 cup

Almond	696
Corn	433
Cracker	450
Graham cracker	465
Matzo	444

CHAPTER 4

Cereal, Pancakes, Waffles and French Toast

CEREAL, ready to eat, 1 cup

bran

All-Bran, *Kellogg's*	190
40% Bran Flakes, *Kellogg's*	140
100% Bran Flakes, *Nabisco*	150
40% Bran Flakes, *Post*	125
Bran Chex, *Ralston Purina*	165
Bran & Prune Flakes, *Post*	120
Bran & Raisin Flakes, *General Mills*	125
Raisin Bran, *Kellogg's*	200
Raisin Bran, *Ralston Purina*	200
Raisin Bran, *Safeway*	200

Raisin Bran with Sugar Coating, *Post*   178
Bran-Buds with wheat germ, *Kellogg's*   200

corn

Country Corn Flakes, *General Mills*   80
Kix, *General Mills*   75
Corn Flakes, *Kellogg's*   110
Toasties Corn Flakes, *Post*   110
Corn Chex, *Ralston Purina*   110
Corn Flakes, *Ralston Purina*   110
Corn Flakes, *Safeway*   110
Corn Flakes & Blueberries, *Post*   110
Corn Flakes & Strawberries, *Post*   110
Sugar Frosted Flakes, *Kellogg's*   144
Sugar Pops, *Kellogg's*   105
Honeycomb Corn, *Post*   85
Sugar Sparkled Flakes, *Post*   149
Cocoa Puffs, *General Mills*   110
Trix, *General Mills*   111

corn and oats

Sugar Sparkled Twinkies, *General Mills*   112
Cap'n Crunch, *Quaker*   163
Crisp, *Quaker*   105

oats

Cheerios, *General Mills*   110
OK's, *Kellogg's*   83
Alpha-Bits, *Post*   110
Crispy Critters, *Post*   110
Fortified Oat Flakes, *Post*   165
Life, *Quaker*   160
Lucky Charms, *General Mills*   110

Frosty O's, *General Mills*	110
Sugar Jets, *General Mills*	111
Stars, *Kellogg's*	112
Fruit Loops, *Kellogg's*	112

rice

Rice Krispies, *Kellogg's*	105
Puffed Rice, *Quaker*	45
Crispy Rice, *Ralston Purina*	110
Rice Chex, *Ralston*	110
Crispy Rice, *Safeway*	110
Puffa Puffa Rice, *Kellogg's*	120
Rice Honeys, *Nabisco*	150
Rice Krinkles, *Post*	127
Cocoa Crispies, *Kellogg's*	113

wheat

Buc Wheats, *General Mills*	146
Total, *General Mills*	110
Wheat Stax, *General Mills*	81
Wheaties, *General Mills*	108
Crumbles, *Kellogg's*	140
Pep, *Kellogg's*	106
Shredded Wheat, *Kellogg's* 1 biscuit	63
Shredded Wheat, *Nabisco* 1 biscuit	92
Grape Nuts Flakes, *Post*	150
Puffed Wheat, *Quaker*	38
Shredded Wheat, *Quaker* 1 biscuit	68
Wheat Chex, *Ralston Purina*	165
Sugar Crisp, *Kellogg's*	147
Sugar Smacks, *Kellogg's*	110
Wheat Honeys, *Nabisco*	153

4

mixed grains

Concentrate, *Kellogg's*	310
Product 19, *Kellogg's*	106
Special K, *Kellogg's*	70
Apple Jacks, *Kellogg's*	112
Team Flakes, *Nabisco*	83
Grape Nuts, *Post*	400
Quake, *Quaker*	118

Cereal, cooked, 1 cup

barley
Quaker	172

corn meal mush
Quaker	128

farina

Cream of Wheat
Instant	133
Mix'N Eat	140
Quick	133
Regular	133
H-O	168
Pillsbury	120
Quaker	100

grits

Quaker
Instant	79

Instant with cheese flavor, 1 pkt	105
Instant with imitation bacon, 1 pkt	100
Instant with imitation ham, 1 pkt	100
3-Minute Brand, ¼ cup	150
oats	
H-O	150
Quaker	160
oatmeal	
Quaker	143
rice	
Cream of Rice	145
rye	
Con Agra	360
whole wheat	
Quaker Pettilohns	145

PANCAKES, FRENCH TOAST, WAFFLES AND OTHER BREAKFASTS, 1 piece unless noted

Breakfast Bars, frozen

Carnation	210
General Mills	190

Crepes, mix, 6″ crepe
 Aunt Jemima   55
French Toast, frozen
 Aunt Jemima   85
  with cinnamon   100
 Downyflake   135
 Swanson, with sausage, 1 pkg   335
French Toast, mix
 McCormick   119
Fritters, frozen
 Mrs. Paul's   120
Pancakes, frozen
 Downyflake   75
 Swanson, with sausage, 1 pkg   500
Pancakes, frozen batter
 Aunt Jemima   70
Pancakes, mix, 4″ pancake
 Aunt Jemima
  Easy Pour   60
  buckwheat   80
  buttermilk   70
 Betty Crocker   70
 Hungry Jack   75
  blueberry   112
  buttermilk   80
  Extra Lights   60
Pancake-Waffle, mix
 Aunt Jemima   70
  buttermilk   100
  whole wheat   80

Log Cabin   60
    buttermilk   75
Waffle, mix
   Aunt Jemima   100
   Downyflake   60
    Jumbo   89

CHAPTER 5

Beans, Pasta and Rice

BARLEY, 1 cup

pearled, light	698
pearled, Pot or Scotch	696

BEANS DRIED,
1 cup unless noted

Broadbeans, raw, immature seeds, 8 oz	238
Broadbeans, raw, mature seeds, 8 oz	768

5

Black, dry, uncooked, 8 oz	768
Chick peas	
8 oz	817
1 cup	720
Great Northern	212
Lima, immature seeds	190
Lima, mature seeds, dried	262
Mung, dried	714
Pea or Navy, dried	224
Pinto (red Mexican), uncooked	663
Red Kidney	220
White, dried	224

Baked Beans, ½ cup

B & M	180
Campbell	148
barbecue	171
with franks	181
with pork	147
Heinz	140
Campside	180
with franks	184
with pork	150
Howard Johnson's	163
Morton House	160

PASTA, 1 cup unless noted

Dry

egg noodles

Goodman's	175
La Rosa	190
La Rosa spinach	200
Pennsylvania Dutch	200
Prince	190
Ronzoni	200

macaroni

Goodman's	170
La Rosa	180
Prince	170
Ronzoni	175

spaghetti

Buitoni	175
Goodman's	160
La Rosa	165
Prince	160
Ronzoni	165

5

Macaroni, canned, bagged, frozen and mixes

with beef

Banquet	260
Chef Boy-Ar-Dee	235
Franco-American	220
Green Giant Boil-in-Bag, 1 pkg	240
Morton	260
Stouffer's, 1 pkg	380

with beef and cheese

Banquet	300
Green Giant Boil-in-Bag, 1 pkg	330
Hormel, 7½ oz can	340
Howard Johnson's	330
Morton	215
Mac-A-Roni & Cheddar	290
Pennsylvania Dutch	310
Stouffer's, 1 pkg	520
Swanson	200

with cheese sauce

Franco-American	225
Heinz	230
MacaroniO's	180
Noodle-Roni	290
Scallop-A-Roni	275

with chili sauce

Fiesta Mac-A-Roni	270

creole style

Heinz, 8¾-oz can	169

Noodles, canned, frozen and mixes

Almondine
   Betty Crocker, 1 pkg   960
with beef
   Heinz, 8½ oz can   170
with beef in gravy
   College Inn   238
with beef in tomato sauce
   College Inn   238
with beef
   Hormel, 7½-oz can   240
with beef sauce
   Pennsylvania Dutch   260
   Betty Crocker   170
with butter sauce
   Pennsylvania Dutch   300
with cheese
   Noodle-Roni   650
with cheese sauce
   Pennsylvania Dutch   300
with cheese sauce and sour cream
   Noodle-Roni Romanoff   362
with chicken
   Dinty Moore, 7½-oz can   215
with chicken sauce
   Noodle-Roni   250
   Pennsylvania Dutch   300
   Twist-A-Roni   250

5

Romanoff
Betty Crocker, 1 pkg	800
Stouffer's, 1 pkg	500

Stroganoff
Betty Crocker, 1 pkg	900
Pennsylvania Dutch	630

with tuna
Stouffer's, 1 pkg	400

Noodles, Italian style, canned, frozen and mixes

Cannelloni, 8 oz
Weight Watchers	275

Eggplant Parmigiana, 8 oz
Buitoni	421
Weight Watchers	172

Lasagna, 8 oz unless noted
Buitoni	250
with meat sauce	340
Chef Boy-Ar-Dee	
canned	241
mix	265
Golden Grain, 1 pkg	720
Green Giant	
Boil-in-Bag, 1 pkg	310
Oven Bake, 1 pkg	300
Hormel	
7½-oz can	270
10-oz can	370

Lean Cuisine, 11 oz	260
Lean Line, 10 oz	270
Roman	274
Stouffer's, 1 pkg	385
Swanson, 1 pkg	540
Weight Watchers	215

Manicotti, 8 oz
Buitoni	395
with sauce	350
Lean Line	270

Ravioli, 8 oz
Buitoni	
cheese	575
meat	680
Chef Boy-Ar-Dee	
cheese	263
meat	210
Franco-American, 7½-oz can	220
La Rosa	
cheese	205
meat	218
Roman	
cheese	496
meat	552

Ravioli Parmigiana, 8 oz
Buitoni	
cheese	301
meat	381

5

Rotini
Franco-American, 7½-oz can   200
   with meatballs   230

Shells
Buitoni, 8 oz   235
Lean Line, 11 oz   270

Spaghetti, all with tomato sauce, 1 cup unless noted
Banquet with meatballs   212
Betty Crocker, 1 pkg   170
Buitoni
   with meatballs   250
   with mushrooms   170
Chef Boy-Ar-Dee
   with cheese sauce   180
   with meat   260
   with meat sauce   250
   with meatballs   250
   with mushrooms   225
Franco-American
   with cheese sauce   200
   with meat   290
   with meatballs   260
Spaghetti-Os
   with cheese   200
   with meatballs   228
Golden Grain   275
Green Giant, Boil-in-Bag
   with meatballs   280

Heinz
with cheese sauce	175
with franks	310
with meat sauce	173

Hormel
with meat	280
with meat sauce	205

Kraft	260
La Rosa with meatballs	230
Lean Cuisine	280
Libby's with meatballs	95
Morton, frozen, 1 pkg	220
Stouffer's, 1 pkg	445
Swanson, 1 pkg	290

Ziti
Buitoni, 8 oz	270
Lean Line, 10 oz	270
Weight Watchers, 1 pkg	350

RICE, 1 cup unless noted

Plain
Ann Page, whole pkg	1000
Bird's Eye	260
Carolina –	200

5

Green Giant	230
Minute	300
Rice-A-Roni, whole pkg	780
River	200
Uncle Ben's	200
Uncle Ben's, brown	250

Flavored

beef
Uncle Ben's — 210

beef and cracked rice
Betty Crocker — 416

beef and vermicelli
Minute — 300
Rice-A-Roni — 315

beef and cheese sauce
Betty Crocker — 350

chicken
Uncle Ben's — 210

chicken with crumb topping
Betty Crocker — 365

chicken and vermicelli
Minute — 300
Rice-A-Roni — 321

curry
Uncle Ben's — 205

fried Chinese and vermicelli
Rice-A-Roni — 375

ham and vermicelli
Rice-A-Roni — 300

pilaf
  Uncle Ben's   290
Frozen
  Green Giant   160
    Medley   220
    Pilaf   240
    Verdi   140
Spanish, canned
  Heinz   190
  La Rosa   155
  Libby's   57
  Stokely-Van Camp   180

Bulgur (parboiled wheat), 1 cup

Club Wheat, dry   630
Hard Red Winter Wheat, dry   605
  canned, unseasoned   225
  seasoned   246
White Wheat, dry   555

CHAPTER 6

Soup

CANNED OR FROZEN,
1 cup unless noted

Alphabet
  Golden Grain   55
Alphabet vegetable
  Lipton   68
Asparagus, cream of
  Campbell's   165
Bean
 plain
    Manischewitz   112
    Wyler's   95

with bacon

   Ann Page   140

   Campbell's   174

   Town House   155

with hot dogs

   Campbell's   168

with smoked pork

   Heinz   160

Bean, black

   Campbell's   95

   Crosse & Blackwell   118

Bean, lima

   Manischewitz   93

Beef

plain

   Campbell's   105

   Lipton   200

with barley

   Manischewitz   83

   Wyler's   72

with cabbage

   Manischewitz   62

with low sodium

   Campbell's, 7¼-oz can   170

mushroom

   Lipton   45

with noodles

   Campbell's   69

   Heinz   74

   Manischewitz   65

chicken
  Maggi   7
  Wyler's   6

Broth
beef
  Campbell's   26
  College Inn   15
  Swanson, 6¾-oz can   25
  Weight Watchers, 1 pkt   10
chicken
  Campbell's   43
  College Inn   32
  Richardson & Robbins   17
  Swanson, 6¼-oz can   25
chicken with noodles
  College Inn   45
chicken with rice
  College Inn   45
  Richardson & Robbins   45

Celery, cream of
  Ann Page   60
  Campbell's   160
  Heinz   180
  Town House   100

Cheddar cheese
  Campbell's   150

Chickarina
  Progresso   100

Chicken
  Lipton   220

Campbell's	51
Heinz	58
Lipton	59
Manischewitz	48
Town House	60
Wyler's	49

Chicken with stars

Ann Page	65
Campbell's	60

Chicken with vegetables

Ann Page	80
Campbell's	73
Heinz	85
Lipton	70
Manischewitz	55
Town House	85
Wyler's, mix	28

Chili, with beef

Campbell's	165
Heinz	160
Town House	160

Chowder

clam, Manhattan

Campbell's	77
Doxsee	62
Heinz	74
Howard Johnson's	104
Crosse & Blackwell	75

clam, New England

Campbell's	206

Mushroom

Plain

Campbell's	80
Golden Grain	95
Souptime	80
Wyler's	151

with barley

Manischewitz	72

bisque

Crosse & Blackwell	127

cream of

Ann Page	120
Campbell's	217
Heinz	200
Knorr-Swiss	116
Lipton	92
Town House	124
Wyler's	151

Noodle

Lipton	50

with chicken broth

Ann Page, 1 pkt	225
Lipton	60

with ground beef

Campbell's	98

Onion

Ann Page, 1 pkt	125
Crosse & Blackwell	57
Golden Grain	33

Knorr-Swiss	45
Lipton	35
Souptime, 1 pkt	20
Wyler's	146
Onion with mushroom	
Lipton	35
Oriental style	
Lipton	210
Oyster stew	
Campbell's	
canned	146
frozen	196
Pea	
green	
Campbell's	148
Golden Grain	73
Knorr-Swiss	71
Lipton	136
Souptime low sodium, 1 pkt	70
with ham	
Campbell's	130
low sodium, 7½-oz can	150
split	
Manischewitz	133
split with ham	
Ann Page	180
Campbell's	180
Heinz	150
Town House	154

Pepper pot
  Campbell's   105
Petite Marmite
  Crosse & Blackwell   41
Potato
  Plain
    Lipton   100
  cream of
    Campbell's   190
  with leek
    Wyler's   155
Schav
    Manischewitz   11
    Rokeach   12
Scotch broth
    Campbell's   90
Senegalese
    Crosse & Blackwell   75
Shrimp, cream of
    Crosse & Blackwell   113
    Campbell's   230
Sirloin burger
    Campbell's   177
Steak and potato
    Campbell's   160
Stockpot
  vegetable
    Lipton   220
  vegetable-beef
    Campbell's   96

Tomato
Ann Page 80
Campbell's 84
Heinz 87
Lipton 93
Manischewitz 61
Progresso 110
Souptime, 1 pkt 70
Town House 87

Tomato bisque
Campbell's 126

Tomato
low sodium
Campbell's 7¼-oz can 130
with rice
Ann Page 90
Campbell's 106
Manischewitz 78
with vegetables
Golden Grain 86
Lipton 69

Tuna Creole
Crosse & Blackwell 70

Turkey
Plain
Campbell's 138
with noodles
Ann Page 75

Heinz	83
Lipton	74
Town House	83
low sodium	
Campbell's, 7¼-oz can	60
with vegetables	
Ann Page	60
Campbell's	78
Vegetable	
Plain	
Ann Page	70
Campbell's	83
Old Fashioned	74
Lipton	70
Italian	100
Knorr-Swiss	56
Manischewitz	63
Town House	83
Wyler's	81
with beef	
Ann Page	80
Campbell's	81
low sodium, 7¼-oz can	80
Old Fashioned	79
Heinz	66
Lipton	53
Town House	66
cream of	
Souptime, 1 pkt	80

CHAPTER 7

Meat, Poultry and Seafood

MEAT, FRESH

Retail cuts of meat are frequently weighed with bone first, *then* they are trimmed, cooked and weighed for their yield. So for instance 1 lb. of pork loin chops are weighed raw with bone, but after they are trimmed and cooked, their yield is 5.9 oz.

Beef, choice-grade, retail cuts

Chuck, arm, roast, or steak; boneless, lean with fat
raw, 1 lb	1,012
braised, drained	
10.7 oz (yield from 1 lb)	879
4 oz	328
1 cup, chopped	405
1 cup, ground	318

Chuck, arm, roast, or steak, lean only
braised, drained	
9.1 oz (yield from 1 lb)	498
4 oz	219
1 cup, chopped	270
1 cup, diced	212

Chuck, rib roast or steak, lean with fat
raw, 1 lb	1,597
braised, drained	
10.7 oz (yield from 1 lb)	1,298
4 oz	484
1 cup, chopped	598
1 cup, ground	470

Chuck, stewing; boneless, lean with fat
raw, 1 lb	1,166
stewed, drained	
10.7 oz (yield from 1 lb)	994
4 oz	371
1 cup, chopped	458

Chuck, stewing; boneless, lean only
raw, 1 lb	717

stewed, drained
 10.7 oz (yield from 1 lb)   651
 4 oz   243
 1 cup, chopped   300
Club steak, 16% bone, lean with fat
 raw, 1 lb   1,443
 broiled
  9.8 oz (yield from 1 lb raw)   1,262
  4 oz without bone   515
Club steak, 16% bone, lean only
 broiled
  5.7 oz (yield from 1 lb)   393
  4 oz without bone   277
Flank steak, boneless, lean only
 raw, 1 lb   653
 braised, drained
  10.7 oz (yield from 1 lb)   596
  4 oz   222
Ground, lean with 10% fat
 raw, 1 lb   812
 broiled, 12 oz (yield from 1 lb)   745
Ground, lean with 21% fat
 raw, 1 lb   1,216
 broiled, 11.5 oz (yield from 1 lb)   932
Plate, boneless, lean with fat
 raw, 1 lb   1,216
 simmered, drained
  10.7 oz (yield from 1 lb)   1,313
  4 oz   490

Plate, boneless, lean only
  simmered, drained
    6.5 oz (yield from 1 lb)   368
    4 oz   226
Porterhouse steak, 9% bone, lean with fat
  raw, 1 lb   1,603
  broiled
    10.6 oz (yield from 1 lb)   1,400
    4 oz without bone   527
Porterhouse steak, 9% bone, lean only
  broiled
    6.1 oz (yield from 1 lb)   385
    4 oz without bone   254
Rib roast, boneless, lean with fat
  raw, 1 lb   1,819
  roasted
    11.7 oz (yield from 1 lb)   1,456
    4 oz   499
    1 cup, chopped   616
    1 cup, ground   484
Rib roast, boneless, lean only
  roasted
    7.5 oz (yield from 1 lb)   511
    4 oz   273
    1 cup, chopped   337
    1 cup, ground   265
Round steak, boneless, lean with fat
  raw, 1 lb   894
  braised or broiled
    11.1 oz (yield from 1 lb)   820

4 oz	296
Round steak, boneless, lean only	
braised or broiled	
9.5 oz (yield from 1 lb)	507
4 oz	296
Rump roast, boneless, lean with fat	
raw, 1 lb	1,374
roasted	
11.7 oz (yield from 1 lb)	1,149
4 oz	394
1 cup, chopped	486
1 cup, ground	382
Rump roast, boneless, lean only	
roasted	
8.8 oz (yield from 1 lb)	516
4 oz	236
1 cup, chopped	291
1 cup, ground	229
Sirloin steak, double bone, 18% bone, lean with fat	
raw, 1 lb	1,240
broiled	
9.6 oz (yield from 1 lb)	1,110
4 oz without bone	463
Sirloin steak, double bone, 18% bone, lean only	
broiled	
6.3 oz (yield from 1 lb)	372
4 oz without bone	272
Sirloin steak, round-bone, 7% bone, lean with fat	
raw, 1 lb	1,316

7

broiled

10.9 oz (yield from 1 lb)	1,192
4 oz without bone	439

Sirloin steak, round-bone, 7% bone, lean only
broiled

7.2 oz (yield from 1 lb)	420
4 oz without bone	235

T-bone steak, 11% bone, lean with fat

raw, 1 lb	1,596

broiled

10.4 oz (yield from 1 lb)	1,395
4 oz without bone	537

T-bone steak, 11% bone, lean only
broiled

5.8 oz (yield from 1 lb)	368
4 oz without bone	253

Beef, prepared and specialty cuts

Beef, corned

raw, 1 lb	1,596

cooked

10.7 oz (yield from 1 lb)	1,131
4 oz	422

Beef, dried, creamed, home recipe

8 oz	350

Beef, hearts, lean only
raw

8 oz	245

braised	
4 oz	213
1 cup, chopped	273
Beef, kidneys	
raw, 8 oz	294
braised	
4 oz	286
1 cup, chunks	353
Beef, liver	
raw, 1 lb	635
fried, 4 oz	260
Beef pancreas, raw, 4 oz	
fat	358
medium fat	321
lean	160
Beef suet, raw, 1 oz	242
Beef sweetbreads (thymus)	
yearlings, raw, 1 lb	939
yearlings, braised, 4 oz	365
Beef, tongue	
very fat, raw, trimmed, 8 oz	615
fat, raw, trimmed, 8 oz	524
medium-fat, raw, trimmed	
8 oz	470
braised, 4 oz	277
Beef, tripe, 4 oz	
commercial	113
pickled	70

Lamb, fresh

Leg, lean with fat

raw, with bone, 1 lb	845
roasted, with bone	
9.4 oz (yield from 1 lb)	745
raw, boneless, 1 lb	1,007
roasted, boneless	
11.2 oz (yield from 1 lb)	887
4 oz	317
1 cup, chopped	391

Leg, lean

roasted, with bone	
7.8 oz (yield from 1 lb with fat)	411
roasted, boneless	
9.7 oz (yield from 1 lb with fat)	491
4 oz	211
1 cup, chopped	260

Loin chops, with bone, lean with fat

raw, 1 lb	1,146
broiled	
10.1 oz (yield from 1 lb)	1,023
4 oz	407
1 chop, 3.4 oz	341
1 chop, 2.5 oz	255

Loin chops, with bone, lean only

broiled	
6.9 oz (yield from 1 lb)	368
4 oz	213
1 chop, 2.3 oz	122

1 chop, 1.7 oz	92
Rib chops with bone, lean with fat	
raw, 1 lb	1,229
broiled	
9.5 oz (yield from 1 lb)	1,091
4 oz	462
1 chop, 3.1 oz	362
1 chop, 2.4 oz	273
Rib chops with bone, lean only	
broiled	
6 oz (yield from 1 lb)	361
4 oz	239
1 chop, 2 oz	120
1 chop, 1.5 oz	91
Shoulder, lean with fat	
raw with bone, 1 lb	1,082
roasted, with bone	
9.5 oz (yield from 1 lb)	913
raw, boneless, 1 lb	1,275
roasted, boneless	
11.2 oz (yield from 1 lb)	1,075
4 oz	383
1 cup, chopped	473
Shoulder, lean only	
roasted, with bone	
7 oz (yield from 1 lb)	410
roasted, boneless	
8.3 oz (yield from 1 lb)	482
4 oz	233
1 cup, chopped	287

Lamb's quarters

raw, trimmed, 1 lb	195
boiled, drained	
4 oz	36
1 cup	64

Lamb hearts

raw, 8 oz	368
braised	
4 oz	295
1 cup, chopped	377

Lamb kidneys

raw, 8 oz	238

Lamb liver

raw, 1 lb	617
broiled, 4 oz	296

Lamb tongue

raw, trimmed, 8 oz	452
braised, 4 oz	288

Lamb sweetbreads (thymus), 4 oz

raw	106
braised	200

Ham, retail cuts (see also Pork)

Boiled, 8 oz (about 8 slices)	531
Fresh, lean with fat	
raw, 1 lb with bone and skin	1,188

baked
    9.2 oz (yield from 1 lb)   980
raw, 1 lb without bone and skin   1,397
baked
    10.9 oz (yield from 1 lb)   1,152
    4 oz   424
    1 cup, chopped   524
    1 cup, ground   411

Fresh, lean only
  baked, with bone and skin
    6.8 oz (yield from 1 lb)   421
  baked, without bone and skin
    8.1 oz (yield from 1 lb with fat)   495
    4 oz   246
    1 cup, chopped   304
    1 cup, ground   239

Light-cured, lean with fat
  raw, with bone and skin, 1 lb   1,100
  baked, with bone and skin
    11.3 oz (yield from 1 lb)   925
  raw, without bone and skin, 1 lb 1,279
  baked, without bone and skin
    13.1 oz (yield from 1 lb)   1,075
    4 oz   328
    1 cup, chopped   405
    1 cup, ground   318

Light-cured, lean only
  baked, with bone and skin
    8.7 oz (yield from 1 lb with fat)   460

baked, without bone and skin
10.2 oz (yield from 1 lb with fat)   539
baked, without bone and skin
4 oz   328
1 cup, chopped   405
1 cup, ground   318

Long-cured, dry, unbaked
medium-fat, lean with fat, with bone and skin,
4 oz   384
lean, lean with fat, with bone and skin, 4 oz   302

Ham, minced, 4 oz   259

Pork, fresh

Boston butt, shoulder, with bone and skin, lean with fat
raw, 1 lb   1,220
roasted, 10.2 oz (yield from 1 lb)   1,024
Boston butt, shoulder, without bone and skin, lean with fat
raw, 1 lb   1,302
roasted
10.9 oz (yield from 1 lb)   1,087
1 cup, chopped   494
1 cup, ground   388
Boston butt, shoulder, with bone and skin, lean only
roasted, 8.1 oz (yield from 1 lb with fat)   559

Boston butt, shoulder, without bone and skin, lean only
  roasted

8.6 oz (yield from 1 lb with fat)	595
1 cup, chopped	342
1 cup, ground	268

Loin chops, with bone, lean with fat
  raw, 1 lb   1,065
  broiled

8.2 oz (yield from 1 lb)	911
1 chop, 2.7 oz	305
1 chop, 2 oz	227

Loin chops without bone, lean with fat
  raw, 1 lb   1,352
  broiled

10.4 oz (yield from 1 lb)	1,153
4 oz	411

Loin chops, with bone, lean only
  broiled

5.9 oz (yield from 1 lb with fat)	454
1 chop, 2 oz	151
1 chop, 1.5 oz	113

Loin chops, without bone, lean with fat

raw, 1 lb	1,065
baked or roasted, 8.6 oz (yield from 1 lb)	883

Loin roast, without bone, lean with fat
  raw, 1 lb   1,352
  baked or roasted

10.9 oz (yield from 1 lb)	1,115
4 oz	411
1 cup, chopped	507

Loin roast, with bone, lean only
  baked or roasted
    6.9 oz (yield from 1 lb with fat)   495
    1 cup, chopped   356
Loin roast, without bone, lean only
  baked or roasted
    8.7 oz (yield from 1 lb with fat)   627
    4 oz   288
    1 cup, chopped   356
Picnic, shoulder, with bone and skin, lean with fat
  raw, 1 lb   1,083
  simmered, 8.4. oz (yield from 1 lb)   890
Picnic, shoulder, without bone and skin, lean with fat
  raw, 1 lb   1,315
  simmered
    10.2 oz (yield from 1 lb)   1,085
    4 oz   424
    1 cup, chopped   524
Picnic, shoulder, with bone and skin, lean only
  simmered, 6.2 oz (yield from 1 lb with fat)   373
Picnic, shoulder, without bone and skin, lean only
  simmered
    7.6 oz (yield from 1 lb with fat)   456
    4 oz   241
    1 cup, chopped   297
Spareribs, with bone, lean with fat
  raw, 1 lb   976
  braised
    6.3 oz (yield from 1 lb)   792
    4 oz   499

Pork, specialty cuts, hog

Hearts

raw, 4 oz	128
braised, 4 oz	221
braised, 1 cup	283
Kidneys, raw, 8 oz	240

Liver

raw, 1 lb	594
fried, 4 oz	205
Pancreas (Sweetbreads), 4 oz	274
Spleen, raw, 4 oz	122

Tongue, 4 oz

raw, trimmed	244
braised	287

Pork, specialty cuts, pig, 4 oz

Feet, pickled	227
Salt Pork	
with skin	1,137
without skin	888
Stomach, scalded	274

7

Pork, cured, retail shoulder cuts (for other cured cuts see Bacon and Ham)

Boston butt, with bone and skin, lean with fat
    unbaked, 1 lb   1,277
    baked or roasted, 11 oz (yield from 1 lb)   1,030

Boston butt, without bone and skin, lean with fat
    unbaked, 1 lb   1,320
    baked or roasted
        11.8 oz from 1 lb   1,109
        4 oz   374
        1 cup, chopped   462
        1 cup, ground   363

Boston butt, with bone and skin, lean only
    baked or roasted, 9.1 oz (yield from 1 lb with fat) 629

Boston butt without bone and skin, lean only
    baked or roasted
        9.8 oz (yield from 1 lb with fat)   678
        4 oz   276
        1 cup, chopped   340
        1 cup, ground   267

Picnic, with bone and skin, lean with fat
    unbaked, 1 lb   1,060
    baked or roasted, 9.7 oz (yield from 1 lb)   888

Picnic, without bone and skin, lean with fat
    unbaked, 1 lb   1,293
    baked or roasted
        11.8 oz (yield from 1 lb)   1,085
        4 oz   366
        1 cup, chopped   452

1 cup, ground	355
Picnic, with bone and skin, lean only	
baked or roasted, 6.8 oz (yield from 1 lb with fat)	405
Picnic, without bone and skin, lean only	
baked or roasted	
8.3 oz (yield from 1 lb with fat)	496
4 oz	239
1 cup, chopped	295
1 cup, ground	232
Bacon, Canadian	
uncooked, 1 lb	980
fried, drained	
12 oz (approx. yield from 1 lb)	921
4 oz	311
1 slice 3⅜″ wide	58
Bacon, cured	
raw, 1 lb	3,016
fried, drained	
5.1 oz (approx. yield from 1 lb)	860
1 thick slice	72
1 medium slice	43
1 thin slice	30

Veal, fresh, retail cuts

Chuck cuts and boneless for stew, lean with fat	
raw, with bone, 1 lb	628
stewed, with bone, 8.4 oz (yield from 1 lb)	564

raw, without bone, 1 lb	785
stewed, without bone	
10.6 oz (yield from 1 lb)	703
4 oz	267
1 cup, chopped	329

Loin cuts, lean with fat

raw, with bone, 1 lb	681
braised, or broiled, with bone	
9.5 oz (yield from 1 lb)	629
raw, without bone, 1 lb	821
braised or broiled, without bone	
11.4 oz (yield from 1 lb)	758
4 oz	245
1 cup, chopped	328

Plate (breast of veal), lean with fat

raw, with bone, 1 lb	828
braised or stewed, with bone,	
8.3 oz (yield from 1 lb)	718
raw, without bone, 1 lb	1,048
braised or stewed, without bone	
10.6 oz (yield from 1 lb)	906
4 oz	344

Rib roast, lean with fat

raw, with bone, 1 lb	723
roasted, with bone, 8.5 oz (yield from 1 lb)	648
raw, without bone, 1 lb	939
roasted, without bone	
11 oz (yield from 1 lb)	842
4 oz	305
1 cup, chopped	377

1 cup, ground	296

Round with rump (roasts and leg cutlets), lean with fat

raw, with bone, 1 lb	573
braised or broiled, with bone	
8.7 oz (yield from 1 lb)	534
raw, without bone, 1 lb	744
braised or broiled, without bone	
11.3 oz (yield from 1 lb)	693
4 oz	245
1 cup, chopped	302

Veal, specialty cuts

Calf hearts

raw, 4 oz	140
braised, 4 oz	236
1 cup	302
Calf kidneys, raw, 8 oz	256

Calves' liver

raw, 4 oz	212
fried, 4 oz	296
Calf pancreas, 4 oz, raw	183

Calf tongue, 4 oz

raw, trimmed	143
braised	181

Calf sweetbreads (thymus), 4 oz

raw	106
braised	192

7

Cold Cuts, Sausages and other meats

Beaver, roasted, 8 oz.	563
Bockwurst	
1 lb (approx 7 links)	1,198
1 link (approx 2.3 oz)	172
Bologna	
without binders	
chub, 1 slice (3" x ⅛")	36
ring, 12 oz ring (15" x 1⅜")	942
sliced, 1 slice (approx 1 oz)	79
with cereal	
chub, 1 slice	34
ring, 12 oz ring	891
sliced, 1 slice	74
Brains, all types, fresh, raw, 8 oz	284
Capicola	
1 oz	141
1 slice	105
Cervelat, dry	
1 oz	128
4 slices	54
Frankfurter's without binders	
1 lb	1,343
1 frank (5" x ¾")	133
Frog's legs, raw	
whole, with bone, 1 lb	215
meat only, 4 oz	83
Meat Loaf, 4 oz	227

Muskrat, roasted, 4 oz	174
Rabbit, domesticated	
raw, whole, ready to cook, 1 lb	581
raw, meat only, 4 oz	184
stewed	
whole 8.6 oz (yield from 1 lb)	529
meat only	
4 oz	245
1 cup, chopped	302
1 cup, ground	238
Rabbit, wild	
whole, ready to cook, 1 lb	490
meat only, 4 oz	153
Raccoon, roasted, meat only, 4 oz	290
Reindeer, raw, lean meat only, 4 oz	144
Salami	
dry roll	
8¼ oz roll	1,053
1 slice	23
dry slice	
4 oz	509
1 slice	45
cooked	
8 oz	706
1 slice approx 1 oz	88
Sausage	
Blood pudding	
4 oz	447
1 slice	32

7

Polish

4 oz	345

pork, raw

2 oz patty	284
1 oz link (4″ x ⅞″)	141

pork, cooked

4 oz	543
1 patty	129
1 link	62

scrapple

4 oz	244
1 slice (9/10 oz)	54

souse

4 oz	205
1 slice (1 oz)	51

Sheep tongue

raw, trimmed, 8 oz	602
braised, 4 oz	366

Snails, raw, 4 oz

meat only	103
Giant African, meat only	83

Spleen, all types, 4 oz 125

Terrapin (diamondback), raw

in shell, 1 lb	106
meat only, 4 oz	126

Thuringer cervelat (summer sausage)

8 oz	697
1 slice (approx 1 oz)	87

Turtle, green, raw

in shell, 1 lb	97

meat only, 4 oz	101
Venison, raw, lean meat only, 4 oz	143

MEAT, COMMERCIALLY PACKAGED

Cured and processed meat, 1 oz unless noted

Bacon, cooked, 1 slice	
Hormel	
Black Label	35
Range Label	45
Red Label	37
Oscar Mayer	40
Swift	40
Bacon bits	
Wilson	140
Beef, chopped	
Eckrich, 1 slice	40
Wilson	91
Beef, corned	
Dinty Moore	65
Libby's	101
Safeway	35

Beef, corned brisket
Swift   80
Wilson   45
Beef, dried
Swift   42
Beef, roast
Wilson   33
Beef, smoked
Safeway   35
  · spicy   40
Beef steaks
Hormel   92
Bologna, 1 slice
Eckrich   90
  thick-sliced   160
Hormel   95
Swift   87
Wilson   87
Beef bologna
Eckrich   95
  Beef Smorgas   70
Oscar Mayer   70
Coarse ground bologna
Hormel   75
Fine ground bologna
Hormel   80
Garlic bologna
Eckrich   95
Braunschweiger
Oscar Mayer   100

Wilson	90

Frankfurters, 1 frank

Eckrich	120
Jumbo	190
Skinless	150
Hormel	180
Wieners	105
Oscar Mayer	140
Wilson	140

Beef frankfurters, 1 frank

Eckrich	150
Jumbo	190
Hormel	
Wieners	105
Wranglers	160
Oscar Mayer	140
Vienna	130
Wilson	136

Ham, lunch meat
cooked

Eckrich, 1 slice	40
Hormel	35
Safeway	50
Oscar Mayer, 1 slice	30

chopped

Hormel	70
Oscar Mayer, 1 slice	65

chopped, smoked

Eckrich	40

Ham, whole, canned, 1 oz

Amber	110
Oscar Mayer	32
Swift	63
Wilson	
boned and rolled	56
fully cooked	48
Tender Made	44

Ham, whole, packaged, 1 oz

Hormel	
bone-in	52
Cure 82	48
Curemaster	35
Oscar Mayer	36
Swift	43
Wilson	48

Ham steaks, 1 slice

Oscar Mayer	70

Ham patties, 1 patty

Hormel	200
Swift	250

Ham and Cheese Loaf, 1 slice

Oscar Mayer	75

Honey Loaf, 1 slice

Eckrich	45
Oscar Mayer	40

Liver, beef

Swift	54

Liver cheese, 1 slice

Oscar Mayer	110

Old Fashioned Loaf, 1 slice
Eckrich   75
Oscar Mayer   65
Olive Loaf, 1 slice
Oscar Mayer   65
Pastrami, 1 slice
Eckrich   47
Safeway   40
Pepperoni
Hormel   140
Swift   150
Pickle Loaf, 1 slice
Eckrich   85
Oscar Mayer   65
Polish Sausage
Eckrich   100
Frito-Lay   73
Hormel   80
Pork Butt
Wilson   72
Pork Loin
Eckrich   47
Pork Steaks
Hormel   73
Salami
Hormel   327
Oscar Mayer, 1 slice   50
Sausage, beef
Eckrich   95

7

Sausage, pork
Hormel 95
Wilson 135

Sausage links, 1 sausage
Hormel
  Brown 'n Serve 78
  Little Sizzlers 67
  Midget Links 112
Oscar Mayer 65
Swift 75

Sausage links, smoked, 1 sausage
Eckrich 190
  skinless 115
  Smok-Y-Links 75
Hormel 92
Oscar Mayer 140

Scrapple
Oscar Mayer 45

Sizzlean
Swift 50

Spam
Hormel 85

Summer Sausage
Swift 90

Thuringer
Hormel 100

Tripe
Libby's canned 35

Veal Steaks
  Hormel   35
    breaded   60
Vienna Sausage, 1 sausage
  Hormel   52
  Libby's   84
    with barbecue sauce   76

Canned Meat Entrees, 1 can, various sizes

Beef with barbecue sauce
  Morton House   240
Beef, corned with cabbage
  Hormel   150
Beef Goulash
  Hormel   240
Beef sliced with gravy
  Morton House   190
Chili con carne
  Hormel   340
  Libby's   130
  Morton House   340
Chili con carne with beans
  A&P   440
  Hormel   320
  Libby's   180
  Morton House   340
  Swanson   310
Hash, beef with potatoes
  Dinty Moore   270

Hash, corned beef
Ann Page	400
Armour Star	435
Bounty	405
Broadcast	480
Libby's	160
Morton House	480
Wilson	480

Hash, roast beef
Hormel	375

Meatballs in gravy
Chef Boy-Ar-Dee	315

Pork, sliced with gravy
Morton House	190

Salisbury Steak with mushroom gravy
Morton House	160

Sloppy Joe
Banquet	250
Gebhardt	280
Hormel	365
Libby's	
beef	163
pork	139

Stew, beef
Armour Star	200
B & M	163
Bounty	213
Dinty Moore	184
Heinz	253
Morton House	312

7

James River Smithfield	186
Libby's	78
Morton House	240
Swanson	190
Wilson	202

Stew, lamb
B & M	247

Stew, meatball
Chef Boy-Ar-Dee	218
Libby's	121
Morton House	290

Stew, Mulligan
Dinty Moore	240

Frozen Meat Entrees, 1 whole package, various sizes (see also pp 385-391, Frozen Dinners)

Beef
Banquet
Cookin' Bag	124
Buffet Supper, 32 oz	782
Green Giant Boil-in-Bag	130
Seabrook Farms	263
Stouffer's	235
Swanson	190
Swanson Hungry-Man	330

Beef goulash
Seabrook Farms — 198

Beef Pot Pie
Banquet — 412
Swanson — 443

Beef Stroganoff
Stouffer's — 390

Green Pepper Steak
Stouffer's — 350

Meat Loaf
Banquet
   Buffet Supper, 32 oz — 1,445
   Cookin' Bag — 224
   Man Pleaser — 916
Morton — 430
Swanson — 330

Noodles and Beef
Banquet Buffet Supper, 32 oz — 754

Salisbury Steak
Banquet — 873
Green Giant Boil-in-Bag — 390
Morton — 490
Stouffer's — 500
Swanson — 370
Swanson Hungry-Man — 640

Salisbury Steak with gravy
Banquet
   Buffet Supper, 32 oz — 1,454
   Cookin' Bag — 246

Green Giant Oven Bake	290
Sausage, cheese, and tomato pie	
Weight Watchers	390
Sloppy Joe	
Banquet Cookin' Bag	199
Green Giant Boil-in-Bag	160
Steak	
Weight Watchers	390
Stew, Beef	
Banquet Buffet Supper, 32 oz	700
Green Giant Boil-in-Bag	160
Lambrecht	432
Seabrook Farms	229
Stouffer's	310
Stuffed Cabbage with beef	
Green Giant Oven Bake	220
Stuffed Green Pepper with Beef	
Green Giant Oven Bake	200

Meat Substitutes, 1 piece or slice

Morningstar Farms	
Breakfast Links	62
Breakfast Patties	111
Breakfast Strips	38

Loma Linda

Bologna	190
Burgers	
Redi-Burger	150
Sizzle Burger	180
Frankfurters	110
Linketts	70
Little Links	45
Meatballs	48
Peanut Butter	
Nuteena	210
Proteena	160
Roast Beef	200
Salami	210
Sausage	
Breakfast Links	50
Breakfast Sausage	140
Swiss Steak	140
Tender Bits	20
Tender Rounds	50
Turkey	190
Vegeburger, 1 cup	240
Vegelona	160

POULTRY, FRESH

Chickens, fresh

Broilers
  broiled, with skin, giblets

7.1 oz (yield from 1 lb)	273
meat only, 4 oz	154
Capon, raw, ready to cook, 1 lb	382

Fryers

raw, ready to cook, 1 lb	382

  fried, with skin, giblets

8 oz (yield from 1 lb)	565

  fried, without skin

dark meat, 4 oz	249
light meat, 4 oz	223
1 back (approx 2 oz)	139
½ breast (approx 3.3 oz)	160
1 drumstick (approx 2 oz)	88
1 neck (approx 2 oz)	127
½ rib section (approx ¾ oz)	41
1 thigh (approx 2.3 oz)	122
1 wing (approx 1.8 oz)	82
skin only (approx 1 oz)	119

Roasters

raw, ready to cook, 1 lb	791

  roasted, with skin, giblets

8.4 oz (yield from 1 lb)	576

roasted, without skin, dark meat

4 oz	204
1 cup, chopped	258
1 cup, ground	202

roasted, without skin, light meat

4 oz	207
1 cup, chopped	255
1 cup, ground	200

Stewing hens or cocks

raw, ready to cook, 1 lb	987
stewed, with skin, giblets, 8 oz (yield from 1 lb)	708

stewed, without skin, dark meat

4 oz	235
1 cup, chopped	290
1 cup, ground	228

stewed, without skin, light meat

4 oz	204
1 cup, chopped	252
1 cup, ground	198

Chicken gizzards

raw, 1 lb	513

simmered

12 oz (yield from 1 lb)	497
4 oz	168
1 cup, chopped	215

Chicken hearts

raw, 4 oz	152

simmered

4 oz	221
1 cup, chopped	283

Chicken liver

raw, 1 lb	585
simmered	
4 oz	187
1 cup, chopped	231
1 liver 2″ x 2″ x ½″	45

Duck, fresh

Domesticated

raw, meat only, 4 oz	188
roasted, meat only, 4 oz	352

Wild

raw, meat only, 4 oz	157

Goose, fresh, domesticated

raw, whole, ready to cook, 1 lb	1,172
roasted	
whole, 8½ oz (yield from 1 lb)	1,022
meat only, 4 oz	266
meat and skin, 4 oz	503
Goose gizzards, raw, 1 lb	631
Goose liver, raw, 1 lb	826

7

Pheasant, fresh

raw, ready to cook, whole, 1 lb	596
raw, meat only, 4 oz	184

Quail, fresh, raw

whole, ready to cook, 1 lb	686
meat and skin only, 4 oz	196
giblets, 2 oz	100

Squab (Pigeon), fresh, raw

whole, dressed, 1 lb	569
meat only, 4 oz	162
light meat only, 4 oz	143

Turkey, fresh

raw, whole, ready to cook, 1 lb	722
roasted, whole, with giblets and skin 8.6 oz (yield from 1 lb)	644
roasted, dark meat without skin 4 oz	230

1 cup, chopped	284
1 cup, ground	223

roasted, light meat without skin

4 oz	200
1 cup, chopped	246
1 cup, ground	194

roasted, skin only, 1 oz   256

giblets

raw, 4 oz	170
simmered	
4 oz	254
1 cup, chopped	338

gizzards

raw, 1 lb	712
simmered	
12 oz (yield from 1 lb)	659
4 oz	222
1 cup, chopped	284

hearts

raw, 4 oz	169
simmered	
4 oz	245
1 cup, chopped	313

liver

raw, 1 lb	626
simmered	
4 oz	197
1 cup, chopped	244

7

POULTRY, COMMERCIALLY CANNED, FROZEN, OR
PACKAGED: 1 package, various sizes, unless noted (see also pp 385-391, Frozen Dinners)

Chicken

a la King
Banquet	138
Green Giant	170
Lambrecht	585
Stouffer's	330
Swanson	190

Boned
Hormel	110
Richardson & Robbins	328
Swanson	110

Chopped, 1 slice
Eckrich	47

Cacciatore
Seabrook Farms	248

Creamed
Stouffer's	300

Creole
  Weight Watchers   250
Croquette
  Howard Johnson's   505
Divan
  Stouffer's   335
and Dumplings
  Banquet   282
  Morton House, 8 oz   363
  Swanson   230
Escalloped
  Stouffer's   500
Fricasse, 1 cup
  College Inn   240
  Richardson & Robbins   229
Fried
  Banquet   259
  Morton   600
  Swanson   290
Livers with broccoli
  Weight Watchers   220
with Noodles
  Banquet   764
  Green Giant   250
  Howard Johnson   384
  Heinz   186
Pot Pie
  Banquet   412
  Morton   318
  Stouffer's   545

Swanson	430
Swanson Hungry-Man	770
with Rice	
Morton House, 8 oz	460
Smoked	
Safeway, 1 oz	50
Stew, 8 oz	
B & M	168
Bounty	221
Libby's	88
Swanson, 7½ oz	180
White meat with peas and onions	
Weight Watchers	270

Turkey

Boned	
Hormel	90
with Giblet gravy	
Banquet	128
Banquet Buffet Supper	170
Pot Pie	
Banquet	415
Morton	390
Stouffer's	460
Swanson	430
Swanson Hungry-Man	770

Slices
Banquet	98
Banquet Buffet Supper	564
Green Giant	100
Morton Country Table	390
Morton House canned	140
Swanson	260
Swanson Hungry-Man	380

Tetrazzini
Stouffer's	480

Smoked
Eckrich, 1 slice	47
Safeway, 1 oz	50

SEAFOOD, FRESH,
4 oz unless noted

Abalone, raw
in shell	47
meat only	111

Barracuda, Pacific, raw
meat only	129

Bass, black sea, raw
whole	41
meat only	106

7

Bass, all varieties, raw
whole	51
meat only	120

Blackfish, see Tautug

Bonito, raw
meat only	192

Butterfish, raw, meat only
gulf	108
northern	192

Catfish, raw, fillets | 117

Caviar, sturgeon
granular
1 oz	74
1 Tbsp	42

pressed
1 oz	90
1 Tbsp	54

Clams, raw, meat only
hard or round
1 pt	363
8 oz	182
4 cherrystones or 5 littlenecks	56

soft
1 pt	372
8 oz	186

Cod
raw, fillets, 8 oz	176
broiled, with butter	
1 steak	352

4 oz	192
dehydrated, lightly salted	308
1 cup, shredded	158
dried, salted	148
Crab, steamed, 8 oz	
in shell	100
meat only	211
Crab, deviled	
8 oz	427
Crab, Imperial	
8 oz	334
Crayfish, raw	
in shell	10
meat only	82
Croaker, Atlantic	
raw, meat only	109
Croaker, white	
raw, meat only	95
Croaker, yellow	
raw, meat only	101
Cusk	
raw, meat only	85
steamed, meat only	120
Eulachon, see Smelt	
Finnan Haddie	
meat only	117
Flounder, fillets	
raw	89
baked with butter	229

Grouper, raw
  whole   42
  meat only   99
Haddock
  raw
    whole, 1 lb   172
    fillets, 1 lb   360
  fried, breaded, 4 oz   187
Halibut, Atlantic or Pacific
  raw
    whole, 1 lb   268
    fillets, 1 lb   452
  broiled with butter, fillets, 4 oz   199
Herring
  Atlantic, raw
    whole, 1 lb   405
    meat only, 4 oz   200
  Pacific
    raw, meat only, 4 oz   111
    salted (in brine), 4 oz   247
    smoked, 4 oz
      bloaters   222
      hard   340
      kippers   239
Inconnu, raw
  whole   104
  meat only   166
Kingfish, raw
  whole   52

meat only	119
Lake Herring (Cisco), raw	
whole	55
meat only	110
Lake Trout, raw	
whole	70
meat only	190
Ling Cod, raw	
whole	44
meat only	96
Lobster, northern	
in shell, 1 lb	
raw	107
cooked	112
Mackerel, Atlantic	
raw, 1 lb	
whole	468
fillets	866
broiled with butter, fillets,	
13 oz yield from 1 lb	861
4 oz	268
Mackerel, Pacific, raw	
whole	130
meat only	181
Mackerel, salted	345
Mackerel, smoked	248
Mullet, raw	
whole	88
meat only	166

7

Muskellunge, raw

whole	60
meat only	124

Mussels, Atlantic or Pacific, raw

in shell	38
meat only	108

Ocean Perch, Atlantic

raw

whole	31
meat only	100
fried, breaded	258

Ocean Perch, Pacific, raw

whole	29
meat only	108

Octopus, raw — 83

Oysters, raw

Eastern

in shell, 1 lb	30
meat only, 4 oz	75
1 medium	20

Pacific Western

meat only, 4 oz	105
1 medium	55

Oysters, cooked

fried, breaded, 1 medium	25

Pickerel, raw — 95

Perch, raw

white

whole	48
meat only	134

yellow
  whole   40
  meat only   103
Pike, raw
  blue
    whole   45
    meat only   100
  northern
    whole   26
    meat only   100
  walleye
    whole   60
    meat only   105
Pompano, raw
  whole   106
  meat only   188
Porgy, raw   52
  meat only   127
Rockfish
  raw   110
  steamed   115
Roe, raw
  carp, cod, haddock, herring, pike, and shad   148
  salmon, sturgeon, and turbot   236
Sablefish, raw
  whole   90
  meat only   216
Salmon, raw
  Atlantic
    whole   160

meat only	246
King (Chinook) meat only	252
Salmon, smoked	200
Sand Dab, raw	
meat only	89
Sardines, Pacific	
raw, meat only	180
Sauger, raw	
whole	34
meat only	95
Scallops, meat only	
raw	92
steamed	127
Sea Bass, white	
raw, meat only	109
Shad, raw	
whole	92
meat only	192
Sheepshead, Atlantic, raw	
whole	60
meat only	128
Shrimp	
raw, whole	
in shell	72
shelled	100
fried, breaded	250
Skate	
raw, meat only	111
Smelt, raw	
whole	60

meat only	110
Snapper, Red and Gray, raw	
whole	55
meat only	106
Sole, raw	
whole	29
meat only (fillet)	90
Spanish Mackerel, raw	
whole	142
meat only	200
Spot	
raw, meat only	250
Squid	
raw, meat only	95
Sturgeon, meat only	
raw	105
steamed	180
Sturgeon, smoked	170
Sucker, carp	
raw	48
meat only	125
Sucker, white and mullet, raw	
whole	195
meat only	118
Swordfish, meat only	
raw	138
broiled in butter	185
Tautug (Blackfish), raw	
whole	37
meat only	101

Tilefish
  raw
    whole 46
    meat only 90
  baked, meat only 155
Tomcod, raw
  whole 34
  meat only 88
Trout, Brook, raw
  whole 56
  meat only 115
Trout, Rainbow, raw
  meat only 220
Tuna, raw, meat only
  bluefin 165
  yellowfin 150
Turbot, Greenland, raw
  whole 86
  meat only 166
Weakfish
  raw
    whole 66
    meat only 138
  broiled in butter 230
Whitefish, raw
  whole 82
  meat only 177
  smoked 177
Wreckfish
  raw, meat only 130

Yellowtail
  raw, meat only   157

SEAFOOD, CANNED
AND FROZEN

Catfish, ocean
  Gorton's, 1 pkg   286
Clams
  Doxsee
    6 oz   84
    8 oz   112
    12 oz   147
  Howard Johnson's
    5 oz   395
    Croquettes, 1 pkg   608
  Mrs. Paul's 1 cake   180
    Thins, 1 cake   155
    Sticks, 1 stick   48
  Sau-Sea, 1 jar   99
  Snow's   60
Cod, 1 pkg
  fillets
    Gorton's   355
    San Juan   336
    Ship Ahoy   336

sticks

Bird's Eye	552
Gorton's	830

Crab

Gold Seal, 1 can	185
Icy Point, 1 can	215
Mrs. Paul's, 1 cake	60
Pillar Rock, 1 can	216
Ship Ahoy, 8 oz	210
Wakefield's, 6 oz	160

Crepes, 5½ oz

Mrs. Paul's

Clam	280
Crab	240
Scallop	220
Shrimp	250

Croquettes

Howard Johnson's

Shrimp with Newburg Sauce	480

Eel, smoked 185

Vita	402

Fish Au Gratin

Mrs. Paul's 1 pkg	250

Fish cakes, fillets and sticks, 1 piece

Mrs. Paul's	105
Beach Haven	110
Thins	160

Fish and Chips

Swanson, 1 pkg	290

Fish Parmesan
Mrs. Paul's, 1 pkg   220
Flounder
Mrs. Paul's, 1 pkg   110
Weight Watchers, 1 pkg   160
Gelfilte Fish, 1 oz
Manischewitz   23
Mother's   14
Rokeach   19
Haddock au Gratin
Howard Johnson's   315
Haddock fillets
Gorton's, 1 pkg   360
Mrs. Paul's, 1 piece   115
Haddock with stuffing
Weight Watchers, 1 pkg   180
Herring, pickled, 1 oz
Vita   40
Oysters, 1 cup
Bumblebee   172
Perch, fried, 1 piece
Mrs. Paul's   125
Perch, ocean with broccoli
Weight Watchers, 1 pkg   190
Salmon, canned, 1 can
  blueback
    Icy Point
      3¾-oz can   181
      7¾-oz can   376

Coho steak
  Icy Point
    3¾-oz can   162
pink
  Del Monte
    7¾-oz can   310
red
  Icy Point
    1-lb. can   775
  Pillar Rock
    3¾-oz can   181
    7¾-oz can   376
red sockeye
  Del Monte
    7¾-oz can   340
  Bumblebee
    1 cup   286
Sardines, 1 oz
  Del Monte   44
  Underwood
    in mustard sauce   52
    in soya bean oil   62
    in tomato sauce   330
Scallops
  Mrs. Paul's, 3½ oz   210
Seafood combination
  Mrs. Paul's   510
Shrimp
  Bumblebee, 1 can   90

Icy Point, 1 can	148
Pillar Rock, 1 can	148
Mrs. Paul's, 1 oz	57
Sau-Sea, 1 oz	80
Shad Roe	
Bumblebee, 1 can	259
Shrimp and Scallops	
Stouffer's, 1 pkg	400
Sole	
Mrs. Paul's, 4½ oz	160
Ship Ahoy, 1 pkg	310
with peas, mushrooms, and lobster sauce	
Weight Watchers, 1 pkg	200
Tuna, canned in oil, drained	
Bumblebee, 1 cup	334
Chicken of the Sea	
3¼-oz can	224
6½-oz can	447
9¼-oz can	636
12½-oz can	860
Del Monte, 6½-oz can	450
Gold Seal, 5-oz can	278
Icy Point, 5-oz can	278
Pillar Rock, 5-oz can	278
Snow Mist, 5-oz can	278
Van Camp, 6¼-oz can	440
Tuna, canned, solid, in water	
Bumblebee, 1 cup	300
Chicken of the Sea, 7-oz can	216

Tuna, creamed, with peas
   Green Giant Boil-in-Bag   140
Tuna Pot Pies
   Banquet   478
   Morton   385
   Star Kist   397
Turbot with peas and carrots
   Weight Watchers, 1 pkg   280

CHAPTER 8

Fruits and Vegetables

FRESH FRUITS AND VEGETABLES

Acerolas (West Indian Cherries)
  whole, 1 lb   104
  pitted, 4 oz   32
  3 cherries   7
Amaranth
  whole, 1 lb   100
  leaves only, 1 lb   160
Apples
  with skin
    1 lb   242

1 apple (3¼", 2 per lb)	123
1 apple (2¾", 3 per lb)	80
1 apple (2½", 4 per lb)	61
chopped, 1 cup	73
pared	
1 apple (3¼", 2 per lb)	107
1 apple (2¾", 3 per lb)	70
1 apple (2½", 4 per lb)	53
chopped, 1 cup	68
Apples, dehydrated	
uncooked	
8 oz	800
1 cup	355
cooked, sweetened	
8 oz	175
1 cup	195
Apples, dried	
uncooked	
8 oz	625
1 cup	234
cooked, unsweetened	
8 oz	177
1 cup	199
cooked, sweetened	
8 oz	254
1 cup	314
Apricots	
whole	
1 lb	217
1 apricot	18

pitted, halves

1 lb	231
1 cup	79

Apricots, dehydrated

uncooked

8 oz	755
1 cup	330

cooked, sweetened

8 oz	271
1 cup	339

Apricots, dried

uncooked

8 oz	590
1 cup	340
10 medium halves	90

cooked, unsweetened, with liquid

8 oz	195
1 cup	210
cooked, sweetened, 1 cup	329

Artichokes

raw, whole, 1 lb	85
boiled, drained, 1 whole bud	67

Asparagus

raw

whole, 1 lb	66
cuts, 1 cup	35

boiled, drained

1 medium spear	3
cuts, 1 cup	29

8

Avocados, California
whole, 1 lb	589
peeled and pitted, 1 average	370
diced, 1 cup	260
mashed, 1 cup	390

Avocados, Florida
whole, 1 lb	389
peeled and pitted, 1 average	200
diced, 1 cup	190
mashed, 1 cup	300

Bamboo shoots, raw
8 oz	61
1 cup, cuts	40

Bananas
whole
1 large (10″)	119
1 medium (9″)	103
1 small (8″)	83

1 cup
sliced	135
mashed	190

Bananas, dehydrated
flakes, 1 cup	340

Bananas, red
whole, 1 average (7¼″)	118
sliced, 1 cup	135

Bean Sprouts, mung
uncooked
8 oz	80
1 cup	37

boiled, drained	
8 oz	65
1 cup	35
Bean sprouts, soy	
uncooked	
8 oz	105
1 cup	48
boiled, drained	
8 oz	86
1 cup	48
Beet greens	
raw, trimmed, 1 lb	61
boiled, drained	
8 oz	41
1 cup	26
Beets	
raw, trimmed	
1 lb	137
whole, 1 beet (2″)	21
diced, 1 cup	58
boiled, drained	
whole, 1 beet	16
diced, 1 cup	58
sliced, 1 cup	66
Blackberries	
1 lb	250
1 cup	84
Blueberries	
1 lb	260
1 cup	90

8

Broccoli
raw
    whole, 1 lb   90
    trimmed, 1 lb   145
boiled, drained
    8 oz   59
    1 average stalk 6½ oz   47
    cuts, 1 cup   40

Brussel Sprouts
raw
    whole, 1 lb   200
    trimmed, 1 lb   190
boiled, drained
    8 oz   82
    1 cup   55
    1 average sprout   7

Cabbage, Chinese (Celery Cabbage), raw
    whole, 1 lb   62
    trimmed, 1 lb   65
    cuts, 1 cup   11
    strips, 1 cup   8

Cabbage, green
raw
    whole, 1 lb   98
    trimmed, 1 lb   110
    chopped, 1 cup   22
    sliced, 1 cup   17
    ground, 1 cup   36
boiled, drained, 1 cup   30

Cabbage, dehydrated, 1 oz   87

Cabbage, red, raw
  whole, 1 lb — 127
  trimmed, 1 lb — 141
  sliced, 1 cup — 22
Cabbage, savoy, raw
  whole, 1 lb — 98
  trimmed, 1 lb — 109
  sliced, 1 cup — 17
Cabbage, spoon (Bakchoy)
  raw
    whole, 1 lb — 73
    trimmed, 1 lb — 70
    cuts, 1 cup — 11
  boiled, drained, cuts, 1 cup — 24
Cantaloupe
  one 5-inch melon — 95
  cubed, 1 cup — 48
Carambola, raw
  whole, 1 lb — 150
  peeled and seeded, 8 oz — 80
Carissas (Natal plums), raw
  whole, 1 lb — 273
  peeled and seeded, 8 oz — 155
  sliced, 1 cup — 105
Carrot
  raw
    whole, 1 lb — 156
    whole scraped
      8 oz — 95
      1 medium — 21

diced, 1 cup	60
slices, 1 cup	53
boiled, drained, 1 cup	45
Carrot, dehydrated, 1 oz	100
Casaba melon	
whole	61
cubed, 1 cup	45
Cauliflower	
raw	
whole, 1 lb	48
flowerets	
1 lb	120
1 cup	27
chopped, 1 cup	30
boiled, drained, 1 cup	29
Celeriac root, raw	
whole, 1 lb	155
pared, 1 root approx 1 oz	11
Celery	
raw	
whole, 1 lb	58
1 large outer stalk (8″)	7
1 small inner stalk (5″)	3
chopped, 1 cup	20
boiled, drained, 1 cup	22
Chard, Swiss	
raw	
whole, 1 lb	113
1 lb, then trimmed	104

boiled, drained
    leaves and stalks, 1 cup   26
    leaves only, 1 cup   32

Chayote
raw, 1 medium squash   56

Cherimoya, raw
whole, 1 lb   247
peeled and seeded, 8 oz   215

Cherries
sour, red
  whole
    1 lb   213
    1 cup   60
  pitted, 1 cup   90
sweet
  whole
    1 lb   286
    1 cup   82
  pitted
    1 cup   102
    1 average cherry   5

Chervil
raw, 1 oz   16

Chives, raw
whole, 1 lb   128
chopped, 1 Tbsp   1

Coconut, raw
in shell, 1 coconut (4½″ and 27 oz)   1,375
shelled, meat only, 4 oz   392

shredded, 1 cup

loosely packed	277
firmly packed	450

Coconut, dried, shredded

unsweetened

4 oz	750
1 cup	622

sweetened

4 oz	622
1 cup	515

Collards

raw

whole, 1 lb	180
leaves only, 1 lb	205

boiled

leaves only	60
with stems, 1 cup	43

Corn, sweet

raw, on the cob, 1 lb	240

boiled, drained

on the cob, 1 ear (5″)	70
kernels, 1 cup	140

Corn Salad, raw

whole, 1 lb	90
trimmed, 1 lb	95

Crab apples, raw

whole, 1 lb	280
trimmed	309

Cranberries

whole, 1 lb	200

without stems, 1 cup	52
chopped, 1 cup	50
Cranberries, dehydrated, 1 oz	100
Cucumber	
1 lb	65
1 average (7½")	35
sliced, 1 cup	15
Currants	
black	
whole, 1 lb	240
trimmed, 1 cup	60
red or white	
whole, 1 lb	220
trimmed, 1 cup	55
Dandelion greens	
raw, trimmed, 1 lb	205
boiled, drained, 1 cup	
loosely packed	35
firmly packed	70
Dates, domestic	
whole, 1 lb	1,081
pitted, 1 lb	1,243
chopped, 1 cup	488
1 average date	22
Dock (Sorrel)	
raw, whole, 1 lb	89
boiled, drained, 1 cup	38
Eggplant	
raw	
whole, 1 lb	92

diced, 1 cup	50
boiled, drained, 1 cup	38

Elderberries

whole, 1 lb	310
without stems, 8 oz	160

Endive (French or Belgian) bleached (Chicory)

trimmed, 1 lb	68
1 head (6″)	8
1 small leave	½
chopped, 1 cup	14

Escarole

whole, 1 lb	80
large outer leaf	5
small inner leaf	½
chopped, 1 cup	10

Fennel, raw

whole, 1 lb	120
trimmed, 2 oz	15

Figs, raw

whole, 1 lb	360
1 medium (2¼″)	40
dried	
8 oz	620
1 medium (2″)	58

Garlic, raw

whole, 2 oz	68
peeled	
2 oz	80
1 clove	3

Ginger root
whole, 1 lb	205
peeled, 1 oz	14

Green (Snap) Beans, 1 cup   31

Gooseberries
1 lb	177
1 cup	59

Grapefruit
pink
whole, 1 lb	89
sections, 1 cup	80

white
whole, 1 lb	86
sections, 1 cup	80

Grapes
American slipskin: Concord, Delaware, Niagara
whole, 1 lb	197

seeded
1 cup	70
1 grape	2

European close skin: Malaga, Muscat, Thompson
whole, 1 lb	270
seeded, 1 cup	100

seedless
1 cup	107
1 grape	3½

Ground-cherries, raw
whole, 1 lb	220

without husks
1 lb	240
1 cup	74

Guava
whole, 1 lb	275
trimmed, 8 oz	140
1 average	58

Honeydew Melon
whole, 1 lb	94
cubed, 1 cup	56

Jack Fruit
  whole, 1 lb   125
  peeled and seeded, 8 oz   110

Jujubes (Chinese dates)
  fresh
    whole, 1 lb   444
    seeded, 8 oz   238
  dried
    whole, 1 lb   1,160
    seeded, 8 oz   650

Kale
  raw
    whole, 1 lb   129
    without stems, 1 lb   155
    leaves only, 4 oz   80
  boiled, drained
    1 cup   31
    leaves only, 1 cup   44

Kohlrabi
  raw
    whole, 1 lb   96
    pared
      8 oz   65
      diced, 1 cup   40
  boiled, drained, 1 cup   40

Kumquats
  whole, 1 lb   274
  trimmed
    8 oz   150

1 medium	12
Leeks, raw	
whole, 1 lb	123
bulb and lower leaf	
8 oz	116
1 medium	17
Lettuce	
Boston	
whole	
1 lb	47
1 head (5″)	23
1 large, 2 medium or 3 small leaves	2
chopped, 1 cup	8
Iceberg	
whole	
1 lb	56
1 head (6″)	70
1 medium leaf	3
chopped, 1 cup	7
Loose Leaf	
whole	
1 lb	52
3 large leaves	15
chopped, 1 cup	10
Romaine or cos	
whole	
1 lb	52
1 leaf	2
chopped, 1 cup	10

Limes

whole, 1 lb	106
pulp only, 1 lime	19

Loganberries

whole, 1 lb	267
trimmed	
8 oz	140
1 cup	90

Loqats

whole, 1 lb	168
seeded	
8 oz	110
1 medium	6

Mangoes, whole

1 lb	200
1 medium	150
1 cup	110

Mushrooms, raw

whole, 1 lb	123
chopped, 1 cup	20

Mustard Greens

raw	
whole	
1 lb	57
trimmed, 8 oz	70
boiled, drained, leaves only	
8 oz	52
1 cup	32

Mustard Spinach (Tendergreens)

raw, whole, 1 lb	100

boiled, drained	
8 oz	37
1 cup	30
Nectarines, whole	
1 lb	267
1 medium	88
New Zealand Spinach	
raw, whole, 1 lb	86
boiled, drained	
8 oz	30
1 cup	23
Okra	
raw	
whole, 1 lb	140
trimmed, 8 oz	80
boiled, drained, sliced, 1 cup	45
Onions, mature	
raw	
whole, 1 lb	157
trimmed	
8 oz	85
1 medium	40
chopped, 1 cup	65
chopped, 1 Tbsp	4
grated, 1 cup	90
boiled, drained, 1 cup	60
Onions, young green	
whole, 1 lb	157
bulb and top	
trimmed, 1 lb	164

chopped, 1 cup	36
chopped, 1 Tbsp	2
top only, chopped	
1 cup	27
1 Tbsp	2

Onions, Welsh
raw

whole, 1 lb	100
trimmed, 8 oz	78

Oranges
whole

1 lb	162
1 medium	64
diced, 1 cup	103

Papaw
whole

1 lb	290
1 medium	83
peeled and seeded	
8 oz	185
1 cup	210

Papayas
whole

1 lb	120
1 medium	120
peeled and seeded	
8 oz	90
cubed, 1 cup	55

Parsley
  whole, 1 lb 200
  chopped
    1 cup 26
    1 Tbsp 2
  1 sprig 4
Parsnips
  raw, whole, 1 lb 293
  boiled, drained
    diced, 1 cup 100
    mashed, 1 cup 140
Passion Fruit
  whole
    1 lb 210
    1 medium 15
  shelled, 8 oz 200
Peaches
  whole, 1 lb 150
  peeled, 1 medium 38
  pared, diced, 1 cup 70
Pears, 1 pear
  Bartlett 200
  Bosc 85
  D'Anjou 120
Peas, green immature
  raw
    whole, 1 lb 150
    shelled
      1 lb 380
      1 cup 120

boiled, drained

8 oz	160
1 cup	115

Peas, mature, dried

raw

whole

1 lb	1,540
1 cup	680
split, uncoated, 1 cup	700
cooked, split, uncoated, 1 cup	230

Pea Pods (Snow Peas)

whole, 1 lb	228

Pepper, Hot chili, green, raw

whole, 1 lb	120
seeded, 8 oz	85

Pepper, Hot chili, red

raw

whole, 1 lb	400
seeded, 8 oz	145
pods, dried, 1 Tbsp	25

Peppers, Sweet, green, raw

whole

1 lb	80
1 pepper, fancy grade large	35
1 pepper, No 1 grade	15
chopped, 1 cup	33

Peppers, Sweet, red, raw

whole, 1 lb	110
seeded and cored, 8 oz	70
chopped, 1 cup	47

Persimmon
  Japanese or Kaki
    whole, 1 lb   286
    seedless, 1 lb   295
    trimmed, 1 medium   130
  native
    whole
      1 lb   475
      1 medium   32
      trimmed and seeded, 8 oz   65

Pigeon peas
  raw, whole, 1 lb   210
  dried, 8 oz   760

Pineapple
  whole, 1 lb   125
  cubed, 1 cup   80

Pitanga (Surinam Cherries)
  whole
    1 lb   187
    4 medium   10
  pitted, 1 cup   87

Plantains, raw
  whole, 1 lb   390
  peeled, 8 oz   270
  1 banana (10″)   **285**

Plums
  Damson
    whole
      1 lb   272

1 medium	7
pitted, 8 oz	150
Japanese	
whole	
1 lb	205
1 medium	32
pitted, 8 oz	110
Prune type	
whole	
1 lb	320
1 medium	21
pitted, 8 oz	170
Poke Shoot (Pokeberry)	
raw, 1 lb	104
boiled, drained, 1 cup	33
Pomegranate	
whole	
1 lb	194
1 medium	100
Potatoes	
raw	
whole, 1 lb	280
peeled, 1 cup	114
baked in skin	
4 oz	81
1 long	145
boiled in skin	
4 oz	79
1 long	173
1 round	104

boiled, peeled
4 oz	74
1 cup	100

fried, 4 oz	275
hash brown, 4 oz	260

mashed, with milk and butter
4 oz	107
1 cup	137

scalloped, with cheese, 4 oz	118

Prickly Pears, raw
whole, 1 lb	84
peeled and seeded, 8 oz	96

Prunes, dehydrated, uncooked
8 oz	780
1 cup	344

Pumpkin, raw
whole, 1 lb	83
pulp only, 8 oz	60

Purslane leaves
raw, whole, 1 lb	95
boiled, drained, 1 cup	27

Quinces
whole, 1 lb	158
peeled and seeded, 8 oz	130

Radishes, raw
whole
1 lb	49
10 medium	8
sliced, 1 cup	20

Radishes, Oriental

whole, 1 lb	57
without tops, 1 lb	67
pared, 8 oz	45

Raisins, seedless

8 oz	655
1 cup loose	420
1 cup firmly packed	477

Raspberries

black

1 lb	330
1 cup	98

red

1 lb	260
1 cup	70

Rhubarb

raw

whole, 1 lb	33
trimmed, 1 lb	60
diced, 1 cup	20
cooked, sweetened, 1 cup	381

Rose Apples

whole, 1 lb	170
trimmed and seeded, 8 oz	138

Rutabagas

raw

whole, 1 lb	177
trimmed, 8 oz	105
diced, 1 cup	60

boiled, drained
cubes, 1 cup 60
mashed, 1 cup 84
Sapodillas
whole, 1 lb 323
peeled and seeded, 8 oz 202
Shallots, raw
whole, 1 oz 18
peeled
1 oz 20
1 Tbsp 7
Soursop, raw
whole, 1 lb 200
peeled and seeded, 8 oz 149
Soybean curd (Tofu)
4 oz 82
Spinach
raw
whole, 1 lb 85
trimmed
leaves, 1 cup 9
chopped, 1 cup 14
boiled, drained, leaves, 1 cup 41
Squash, summer
raw
whole, 1 lb 85
trimmed, 8 oz 25
diced, 1 cup 35
boiled, drained, 1 cup 30

Squash, winter

raw, whole, 1 lb	150
baked, 8 oz	120

Strawberries, whole

1 lb	161
trimmed, 1 lb	168
1 cup	55

Sugar Apples (Sweetsop)

whole, 1 lb	192
peeled and seeded	
8 oz	220
1 cup	235

Swamp Cabbage

raw	
whole, 1 lb	107
trimmed, 1 lb	132
boiled, drained, 8 oz	48

Sweet Potatoes

raw, whole, 1 lb	420
baked in skin, 4 oz	125

Tamarinds

whole, 1 lb	520
shelled and seeded, 8 oz	540

Tomatoes, green

whole, 1 lb	99

Tomatoes, ripe

raw	
whole	
1 lb	100
1 medium	25

sliced, 1 cup	40
boiled, 1 cup	63
Towel Gourd	
whole, 1 lb	70
pared, 8 oz	40
Turnip Greens	
raw	
whole, 1 lb	107
trimmed, 1 lb	127
boiled	
8 oz	46
1 cup	30
Turnips	
raw	
whole, 1 lb	117
cubed, 1 cup	39
boiled, drained	
8 oz	52
1 cup	36
mashed	53
Vinespinach (Basella), raw, 8 oz	44
Water Chestnuts, Chinese	
raw, whole, 1 lb	276
Watercress	
whole	
1 lb	80
1 cup	7
chopped, 1 cup	24
Watermelon	
whole, 1 lb	54

1 wedge (4″ x 8″)	110
diced, 1 cup	42
Wax (Yellow) Beans	
1 cup	29
Yam Beans, raw	
whole, 1 lb	225
pared, 8 oz	130
Yams, raw	
whole, 1 lb	395
pared, 4 oz	115
Zucchini (see Summer Squash)	

FRUIT,
COMMERCIALLY PACKAGED,
CANNED OR FROZEN,
½ cup unless noted

Apples and Apricots	
Mott's	104
Apples and Cherries	
Mott's	110
Apples and Pineapples	
Mott's	127

8

Apples and Raspberries
Mott's	105

Applesauce
Del Monte	85
Mott's	45
S & W	48
Stokely-Van Camp	90
Tillie Lewis	60
Town House	85

Apricots
Del Monte	100
Libby's	100
Stokely-Van Camp	110
Tillie Lewis	60
Town House	80

Blackberries
S & W	36

Blueberries
Seabrook Farms	45

Boysenberries
S & W	32

Cherries
Del Monte Light	95
Dark	90
Dark pitted	95
Libby's	100
S & W	50
Stokely-Van Camp	50

Cherries, maraschino
Vita 1 cherry	20

8

Cranberry and Orange
Ocean Spray   100

Cranberry Sauce
Ocean Spray   90

Currants
Del Monte   190

Dates
Bordo   330
Dromedary   397
Dromedary pitted   376

Figs
Del Monte   100
S & W, 6 figs   49

Fruit Cocktail
Del Monte   85
Dole   72
Libby's   75
S & W   35
Stokely-Van Camp   95
Tillie Lewis   50
Town House   85

Fruit Salad
Del Monte   85
Del Monte Tropical   100
Kraft   48
Libby's   90
S & W   35
Stokely-Van Camp   95

Fruits and Peels
Liberty   388

Grapefruit sections
Del Monte   45
Kraft   43
S & W   36
Tillie Lewis   45

Mixed Fruit
Birds Eye   105

Melon Balls
Birds Eye, 1 pkg   144

Oranges
Del Monte   75
Kraft   52
S & W   27

Peaches
Birds Eye   72
Del Monte   85
Highway   70
S & W   25
Scotch Buy   70
Seabrook Farms   105
Stokely-Van Camp   90
Town House, heavy syrup   95
Town House, extra heavy syrup   130

Peaches and Strawberries
Birds Eye   80

Pears
Del Monte   80
Libby's   85
Libby's Juice Pack   75
Highway   80

Scotch Buy	70
S & W	28
Stokely-Van Camp	105
Tillie Lewis	50

Pineapple

Del Monte in juice	70
Del Monte in syrup	95
Dole in juice	65
Dole in syrup	85
S & W	50
Town House in juice	75
Town House in syrup	95

Plums

Del Monte	95
Libby's	105
S & W	50
Stokely-Van Camp	120
Tillie Lewis	70

Prunes

Del Monte	115
Heart's Delight	210
Sunsweet	196

Raspberries

Birds Eye	120
Seabrook Farms	120

Rhubarb

Birds Eye	138

Strawberries

Birds Eye	90
Birds Eye slices	145

Seabrook Farms	42
Seabrook Farms slices	140
S & W	20

VEGETABLES, COMMERCIALLY PACKAGED, CANNED OR FROZEN,
1 cup unless noted

Artichoke Hearts
Birds Eye	53

Asparagus, cuts
Green Giant	40
Kounty Kist	40
Lindy	39
Stokely-Van Camp	44

Asparagus, Spears
Del Monte	35
Green Giant	40
Le Sueur	38
S & W	18
Town House	35

Asparagus, frozen
Birds Eye	61
with Hollandaise Sauce, 1 pkg	290

Green Giant	90
Seabrook Farms	46
Bamboo Shoots	
Chun King	30
La Choy	23
Bean Sprouts	
Chun King	40
La Choy	24
Beets, cut	
Del Monte	70
Libby's	70
Stokely-Van Camp	90
Beets, diced	
Comstock	82
Libby's	70
Stokely-Van Camp	70
Beets, Harvard	
Greenwood	104
Libby's	160
Lord Mott	80
Stokely-Van Camp	160
Beets, pickled	
Del Monte	150
Greenwood	150
Libby's	150
Lord Mott	150
Stokely-Van Camp	190
Town House	145
Beets, sliced	
Del Monte	70

Libby's	70
Lord Mott	50
S & W	56
Stokely-Van Camp	80
Beets, whole	
Del Monte	70
Libby's	70
Stokely-Van Camp	85
Beets, frozen	
Birds Eye	105
Broccoli, frozen	
Birds Eye	25
with cheese	110
in hollandaise	200
Green Giant	30
in butter	90
in cheese sauce	130
with cauliflower and carrots	140
Kounty Kist	30
Seabrook Farms	46
Stouffer's Au gratin	340
Brussels Sprouts	
Birds Eye	30
Green Giant	50
in butter sauce	110
in cheese sauce	170
Kounty Kist	50
Seabrook Farms	76
Cabbage	
Greenwood	150

Lord Mott	120

Carrots, diced

Comstock	48
Del Monte	61
Libby's	40
S & W	44
Stokely-Van Camp	60

Carrots, sliced

Birds Eye, in buttersauce	340
in sugar	194
Comstock	35
Del Monte	58
Green Giant, in butter sauce	100
Libby's	42
Lord Mott	50
Stokely-Van Camp	50

Cauliflower

Birds Eye	61
with cheese sauce	130
Green Giant	30
with cheese sauce	130
Kounty Kist	26
Seabrook Farms	26

Collard Greens

Birds Eye	30
Seabrook Farms	44

Corn, Yellow, canned

cream style

Birds Eye	170
Del Monte	210

Green Giant	210
S & W	168
Stokely-Van Camp	210
liquid pack	
Del Monte	170
Green Giant	160
Kounty Kist	180
Le Sueur	170
Libby's	160
S & W	104
Stokely-Van Camp	180
vacuum pack	
Del Monte	200
Green Giant	160
Kounty Kist	160
Stokely-Van Camp	240
with peppers	
Del Monte	190
Green Giant	150
Corn, Yellow, frozen	
Birds Eye in butter sauce	200
Green Giant in butter sauce	190
with peppers	180
Stouffer's, 1 pkg	465
Corn, White, frozen and canned	
Birds Eye creamed	170
with peas	140
Del Monte creamed	190
kernels	150
Green Giant	130

8

Kounty Kist	140
Eggplant Parmesan	
Mrs. Paul's	364
Eggplant slices	
Mrs. Paul's	613
Eggplant sticks	
Mrs. Paul's	254
Kale	
Seabrook Farms	60
Mixed Vegetables, canned	
Del Monte	79
La Choy	35
Libby's	78
Stokely-Van Camp	81
Town House	88
Mixed Vegetables, frozen	
Birds Eye	145
Chun King	23
Green Giant	90
Kounty Kist	89
California	30
La Choy	23
Mixed Vegetables, frozen, Chinese style	
Birds Eye Cantonese	123
Birds Eye International	48
Green Giant	130
La Choy	72
Mixed Vegetables, frozen, European styles	
Birds Eye	
Danish	74

Italian	98
Parisian	74

Mixed Vegetables, frozen, Hawaiian style

Birds Eye	98
Green Giant	197

Mixed Vegetables, frozen, Japanese style

Birds Eye	98
Birds Eye with seasonings	74
Green Giant	130
La Choy, 1 pkg	71

Mixed Vegetables, frozen, American styles

Birds Eye

New England	150
New Orleans Creole	150
Jubilee	250
Pennsylvania Dutch	98
San Francisco	111
Wisconsin	111
Green Giant	130

Mushrooms

Birds Eye	50
Brandywine	30
B & B	60
Dole	5
Green Giant	15

Mustard greens

Birds Eye	44
Seabrook Farms	42

Okra

Birds Eye	61

Green Giant	211
Seabrook Farms	52
Onions	
Birds Eye	64
in cream sauce	239
whole	98
Green Giant	140
Lord Mott	60
in cream sauce	130
Ore-Ida	80
Seabrook Farms	232
Onion Rings, 1 oz	
Birds Eye	170
Mrs. Paul's	60
O & C	178
Ore-Ida	80
Peas, canned	
early	
Del Monte	110
Kounty Kist	139
Le Sueur	110
Lindy	138
Lord Mott	110
Minnesota Valley	109
Stokely-Van Camp	128
sweet	
Del Monte	101
Green Giant	110
with onion	105
Kounty Kist	131

Libby's	121
Lindy	130
S & W	70
Stokely-Van Camp	130
with carrots	
Del Monte	100
Libby's	101
Lord Mott	165
S & W	65
Stokely-Van Camp	120

Peas, frozen

early	
Birds Eye	169
Green Giant	102
Kounty Kist	119
Le Sueur	149
Seabrook Farms	148
sweet	
Birds Eye	155
Green Giant	150
Seabrook Farms	104
with carrots	
Birds Eye	122
Kounty Kist	90
Seabrook Farms	82
with cream sauce	
Birds Eye	369
Green Giant	300
with cream sauce and cauliflower	
Birds Eye	247

in onion sauce
   Seabrook Farms   192
with onions
   Birds Eye   149
with onions and carrots
   Le Sueur   180
with potatos
   Birds Eye   431
with mushrooms
   Birds Eye   155

Peppers, green
   Stouffers, 1 pkg   225
   Weight Watchers, one 13-oz pkg   320

Potatoes, canned
   Del Monte   **90**
   Hormel au gratin, 7½-oz can   **270**
      with ham, 7½-oz can   **255**
   Stokely-Van Camp   **103**

Potatoes, frozen, 3 oz unless noted
   Au gratin
      Green Giant, 1 cup   **390**
      Stouffer's   **270**
   French fried
      Birds Eye
         Crinkle Cuts   124
         Cottage Fries   120
         Gold Crinkle Cuts   140
         French   111
         Shoestrings   138
         Steak Fries   109

Ore-Ida	
Cottage Fries	140
Golden Crinkles	130
Sizzling Fries	157
Sizzling Crinkles	171
Sizzling Shoestrings	218
Shoestrings	170
Hash browns	
Birds Eye	54
O'Brien	45
Ore-Ida	70
in butter sauce	120
in butter sauce and onions	130
with parsley	
Seabrook Farms	208
Scalloped	
Stouffer's	252
Shredded hash browns	
Birds Eye	60
Ore-Ida	60
Slices	
Green Giant	210
with sour cream	
Green Giant	270
Stuffed	
Green Giant	
with cheese, 5 oz	240
with sour cream, 5 oz	229
with peas	
Green Giant	242

Taters and Puffs
Birds Eye Tasti Fries 140
Tasti Puffs 190
Ore-Ida Tater Tots 160
Tater Tots with Bacon 151
Tater Tots with Onion 165

With Vermicelli
Green Giant 399

Whole
Birds Eye 179
Ore-Ida 70
Seabrook Farms 153

Potatoes, mix, ½ cup
French's 120
Big Tate 129
Hungry Jack 160

Julienne
Betty Crocker 132

Au gratin
Betty Crocker 150
French's 190

Creamed
Betty Crocker 163

Hash browns
Betty Crocker 147
French's 160

Pancakes
French's 3 cakes 130

Potato Buds
Betty Crocker 132

Scalloped
  Betty Crocker 150
  French's 189
With sour cream
  Betty Crocker 144

Pumpkin
  Del Monte 79
  Libby's 80
  Stokely-Van Camp 88

Sauerkraut
  Del Monte 50
  Libby's 42
  Stokely-Van Camp 50
    Bavarian 69

Soup Greens
  Durkee 213

Spinach, canned
  Del Monte 45
  Libby's 44
  Lord Mott 44

Spinach, frozen
  chopped
    Birds Eye 47
    Seabrook Farms 50
  creamed
    Birds Eye 157
    Green Giant 190
    Lord Mott 130

Seabrook Farms	200
leaf	
Birds Eye	47
Seabrook Farms	48
souffle	
Green Giant	300
Stouffer's, 1 pkg	400
with butter sauce	
Green Giant	89
Squash	
Birds Eye	100
Green Giant	118
Seabrook Farms	92
Stew, vegetable	
Dinty Moore, 7½-oz can	160
Ore-Ida	140
Succotash	
Birds Eye	202
Libby's creamed	190
kernel	151
Seabrook Farms	174
Stokely-Van Camp	170
Sweet Potatoes	
Birds Eye	408
Green Giant	341
Lord Mott	235
Mrs. Paul's	320
Tomatoes	
stewed	70
whole	50

Tomato paste
Contadina   200
Del Monte   200
Hunt's   185
Town House   225
Tomato puree
Contadina   120
Turnip Greens
Birds Eye   47
Seabrook Farms   44
Stokely-Van Camp   46
Zucchini
Birds Eye   39
Del Monte   60
Mrs. Paul's   480

CHAPTER 9

Condiments, Dips, Dressings, Oils and Sauces

CONDIMENTS,
1 Tbsp, unless noted

celery flakes, 1 tsp
Wyler's 7
curry powder
Crosse & Blackwell 26
garlic flavoring, 1 tsp
Burton's 42
garlic powder, 1 tsp
Wyler's 8
garlic spread
Lawry's 88
horseradish
Borden 16
Heinz 26
Kraft 4
Tastee 5
hot sauce, 1 tsp
Frank's 10
Gebhardt 4
Tabasco 4
meat sauces
A-1 12
Crosse & Blackwell 21
Durkee 60
Escoffier 19
Gravymaster, 1 tsp 8
Heinz 57 14
Heinz Savory 21
H.P. 21
Maggi 17

onions, minced, 1 tsp
  Borden's   7
  Wyler's   7
parsley flakes, 1 tsp
  Wyler's   1
pepper
  Seasoned
    Lawry's, 1 tsp   16
  sweet
    Wyler's, 1 tsp   2
salt, flavored, 1 tsp
  celery   6
  garlic   6
  onion   6
sandwich spread
  Hellman's   60
  Kraft   56
vinegar
  Cider or white   1
  Wine
    Holland House
      Marsala   35
      Red   25
      Sherry   40
      White   25
    Regina
      Sauterne   1
      Sherry   10

Flavorings, Extracts, 1 tsp

Almond
Durkee 13
Ehlers 5
Anise
Durkee 16
Ehlers 12
Banana
Durkee 15
Ehlers 7
Black Walnut
Durkee 45
Brandy
Durkee 15
Ehlers 18
Cherry
Ehlers 8
Chocolate
Durkee 8
Coconut
Durkee 7
Ehlers 13
Lemon
Durkee 17
Ehlers 14
Maple
Durkee 6
Ehlers 9

9

Mocha
Durkee   14

Orange
Durkee   16
Ehlers   14

Peppermint
Durkee   15
Ehlers   12

Pineapple
Ehlers   13

Raspberry
Ehlers   10

Rum
Durkee   14
Ehlers   12

Strawberry
Durkee   12
Ehlers   11

Vanilla
Durkee   5

Relishes, Pickles, Olives:
1 piece unless noted

Capers, 1 Tbsp
Crosse & Blackwell   6

Carrots, dill
  Cresca Cocktail Sticks   1

Cauliflower, sweet
  Heinz   9
  Smucker's   23

ChowChow, 1 Tbsp
  Crosse & Blackwell   20

Chutney
  Major Grey's   53

Eggplant
  Cresca   1

Olives
  Green, Manzanilla
    Durkee   4
    Grandee   4
  Green, Spanish
    Vita   11
  Green, queen
    Durkee   14
    Grandee   14
  Ripe
    Durkee   7
    Grandee   7
    Lindsay   6
    Vita   7

Onions
  Cresca   1
  Crosse & Blackwell   1
  Heinz   2
  Heinz Spiced   1

Peppers, 1 oz unless noted
  Chili
    Del Monte   5
    Ortega
      Jalapeños   8
      Green   5
  Hot, 1 pepper
    Cresca   6
    Smucker's   10
  Mild, sweet
    Del Monte   5
  Pickled
    Old El Paso   9
  Red, bell
    Ortega   9
Pickle Relish, 1 Tbsp
  Barbecue
    Crosse & Blackwell   22
    Heinz   31
  Corn
    Crosse & Blackwell   15
  Hamburger
    Crosse & Blackwell   20
    Heinz   17
  Hot dog
    Crosse & Blackwell   22
    Heinz   2
  Hot pepper
    Crosse & Blackwell   22

India
  Crosse & Blackwell 26
piccalilli
  Crosse & Blackwell 25
  Heinz 19
Pickles
  Sour
    Bond's 2
    Crosse & Blackwell 2
    Heinz
      Genuine Dill 10
      Kosher Dills 2
    L & S 2
  Sweet
    Bond's 19
    Crosse & Blackwell 28
      slices, 1 Tbsp 15
    Heinz
      Midget 5
      Sweet Gherkins 25
      Sweet Pickles 45
      Sticks 13
      Candied dill strips 35
Pimientos, 1 oz
  Dromedary 8
  Ortega 7
  Stokely-Van Camp 8
Watermelon Rind, 1 Tbsp 38

Seasonings, 1 tsp unless noted

Accent	9
Bacon	
Ann Page	8
Baco's	13
Durkee	3
French's	2
Lawry's	13
McCormick	
Bits	10
Chips	12
Schilling	
Bits	19
Chips	13
Barbecue	
French's	6
Chili Powder	
Lawry's	9
Mexene	8
Cinnamon Sugar	
French's	16
Chutney	
Major Grey's	16
Spice Island	12
Herb	
Lawry's	9
Horseradish	
Reese	18

Hot Sauce
  Frank's   1
Lemon Pepper
  Lawry's   7
  French's   6
Meat Tenderizer
  French's   2
Pepper
  French's   8
  Lawry's   8
Salad
  Durkee   4
    with cheese   10
  French's   6
Salt
  French's
    Butter   8
    Celery   2
    Garlic   4
    Hickory Smoked   2
    Onion   6
    Parsley Garlic   6
    Seasoned   2
  Lawry's
    Garlic   5
    Onion   4
    Seasoned   1
Seafood
  French's   2

Stock Base
  French's   8

Seasoning Mixes, 1 pkg, various sizes

A la King
  Durkee   297
Beef
  Lawry's
    Beef Olé   126
    Marinade   69
Beef Stew
  Durkee   99
  French's   150
  Lawry's   131
  McCormick   90
  Schilling   89
Beef Stroganoff
  French's   192
  Lawry's   119
  McCormick   113
Beef, Ground
  Ann Page   100
  Durkee   91
  French's   100
Chili
  Ann Page   120
  French's   150

DIPS, 1 oz

Ready to Serve

Bacon and Horseradish
Borden 79
Kraft
  Ready 71
  Teez 57
Lucerne 63
Bacon and Smoke
Sealtest 47
Barbecue
Borden's 48
Bean
  Chili
    Lucerne 50
  Jalapeño
    Frito-Lay 36
    Gebhardt 30
    Granny Goose 37
    Lucerne 35
Blue Cheese
Granny Goose 110
Kraft
  Ready 69
  Teez 51

Lucerne	67
Sealtest	49
Casino	
Sealtest	45
Chili, Green	
Borden	55
Chipped Beef	
Sealtest	44
Clam	
Kraft	
Ready	66
Teez	44
Lucerne	34
Clam and Lobster	
Borden	60
Dill	
Kraft	67
Garlic	
Granny Goose	100
Kraft	47
Lucerne	58
Green Goddess	
Kraft	45
Guacamole	
Lucerne	69
Hickory Smoke	
Lucerne	60
Onion	
Borden	48
Lawry's	50

Unprepared Mixes

Garlic and Onion
McCormick   126
Salada   100
Horseradish
Lawry's   86
Frito-Lay   105
Onion
Frito-Lay   87
Green   100
Lawry's
Green   100
Toasted   82
McCormick   131
Salada   100
Taco
Frito-Lay   105

SALAD DRESSINGS,
1 Tbsp unless noted

Avocado
Kraft   70
Bacon
Lawry's   78
Blue Cheese
Ann Page Low Calorie   18

Kraft
  Chunky   70
  Low Calorie   14
  Low Calorie Chunky   30
Lawry's
  bottled   57
  mix, 1 pkg   74
Nu Made   75
Roka   60
Seven Seas   70
Wish-Bone   80
Weight Watchers   10

Caesar
Kraft   70
Lawry's
  bottled   70
  mix, 1 pkg   72
Nu Made   75
Pfeiffer   70
  Low Calorie   10
Seven Seas   70
Wish-Bone   80

Chef Style
Ann Page   20
Kraft   18

Coach House
Seven Seas   78

Coleslaw
Kraft   70
  Low Calorie   30

9

Cucumber
Kraft 80
  Low Calorie 30
French
Ann Page 25
Casino 70
Kraft 60
  Casino Garlic 70
  Herb and Garlic 90
  Low Calorie 25
  Miracle 70
Lawry's
  bottled 50
  mix, 1 pkg 72
Nu Made
  Low Calorie 20
  Savory 65
  Zesty 70
Pfeiffer 55
  Low Calorie 18
Seven Seas 60
  Low Calorie 30
Tillie Lewis 12
Wish-Bone
  Deluxe 50
  French Garlic 70
  Low Calorie 25
  Sweet and Spicy 70
Weight Watchers 4

Garlic
Kraft   50
Wish-Bone   80

Green Goddess
Kraft   80
Lawry's
  bottled   60
  mix, 1 pkg   69
Nu Made   80
Seven Seas   80
Wish-Bone   60

Green Onion
Kraft   70

Hawaiian
Lawry's   75

Herb and Garlic
Kraft   83

Herb and Spices
Seven Seas   60

Italian
Ann Page   14
Good Seasons   8
Kraft   80
  Golden   70
  Low Calorie   6
Lawry's
  bottled   80
  mix, 1 pkg   44
  cheeses mix, 1 pkg   69

Nu Made	90
Low Calorie	16
Pfeiffer	60
Low Calorie	10
Seven Seas	70
Family	60
Low Calorie	35
Viva	70
Tillie Lewis	6
Weight Watchers	2
Wish-Bone	80
Low Calorie	20
Lemon garlic	
Lawry's, 1 pkg	65
Mayonnaise, all brands	100
Mayonnaise, flavored	
Durkee	69
Mayonnaise, imitation	
Mrs. Filbert's	40
Piedmont	50
Weight Watchers	40
May Lo Naise	
Tillie Lewis	25
Oil and Vinegar	
Kraft	70
Lawry's	55
Nu Made	60
Seven Seasons	70
Onion	
Lawry's	84

Wish-Bone	80
Parmesan	
Good Seasons	84
Roquefort	
Kraft	58
Red Wine	
Pfeiffer	40
Low Calorie	10
Russian	
Kraft	30
Nu Made	55
Pfeiffer	65
Low Calorie	15
Seven Seas	80
Tillie Lewis	12
Weight Watchers	
bottled	50
mix	4
Wish-Bone	60
Low Calorie	25
Salad dressing	
Ann Page	70
Heinz	63
Kraft	65
Mrs. Filbert's	65
Nu Made	80
Piedmont	70
Sultana	50
Salad Secret	
Kraft	60

Sea Island
  Kraft   93
Sour Treat
  Friendship   90
Sherry
  Lawry's   55
Spin Blend
  Hellmann's   55
Tahitian Isle
  Wish-Bone   55
Thousand Island
  Ann Page   25
  Kraft   60
    Low Calorie   30
  Lawry's
    bottled   65
    mix, 1 pkg   78
  Nu Made   30
  Pfeiffer   65
    Low Calorie   15
  Seven Seas   50
  Tillie Lewis   18
  Weight Watchers
    bottled   50
    mix   12
  Wish-Bone   70
    Low Calorie   25
Tomato-Blue Cheese
  Kraft   90

Tomato-Spice
  Seven Seas   45
Whipped
  Tillie Lewis   25
Yogonaise
  Henri's   60
Yogowhip
  Henri's   60
Yogurt, all flavors
  Henri's   35

OILS, 1 Tbsp

Corn
  Mazola   122
  Nu Made   124
Olive
  Filippo Berio   125
Peanut
  Planters   128
Popcorn
  Planters   130
Safflower
  Nu Made   119
Soybean
  Mrs. Tucker's   128

Sunflower
  Sunlight   120
Vegetable
  Crisco   120
  Puritan   118
  Swift   115
  Wesson   120
Vegetable and cottonseed
  Swift   120

Shortening, 1 Tbsp unless noted

Lard   115
  1 cup   1,850
Vegetable
  Crisco   109
  Fluffo   109
  Mrs. Tucker's   120
  Pam   7
  Snowdrift   111
  Spry   97

SAUCES,
½ cup unless noted

A la King
   Durkee   66
Barbecue, 1 Tbsp
   Chris' and Pitt's   15
   Durkee with vinegar   64
   French's   14
      Hot   27
      Smoky   14
   Open Pit   26
      Hot 'n Spicy   27
      Hickory Smoked   27
      with onions   28
Bearnaise
   Butternut Farm   176
Bordelaise
   Butternut Farm   48
Cheese
   Durkee   168
   French's   160
   McCormick   156
   Schilling   156
Chili
   Gebhardt   156
   Heinz   17

Hunt's	18
McCormick	92
Clam	
Buitoni	
red	102
white	114
La Rosa	
red	78
white	68
Cocktail Sauce	
Crosse & Blackwell	26
Tastee	25
Enchilada	
Gebhardt	68
Lawry's, 1 pkg	144
McCormick, 1 pkg	116
Old El Paso	
Hot	36
Mild	40
Hollandaise	
Durkee	118
French's	119
McCormick	171
Schilling	170
Horseradish, 1 oz	
Kraft	100
Italian	
Contadina	85
Lawry's, 1 pkg	86
Ragu	36

Lemon-Butter, 1 oz
Weight Watchers   16
Mint Sauce, 1 tsp
Crosse & Blackwell   16
Mushroom, 1 oz
Dawn Fresh   9
Pizza
Buitoni   92
Ragu   96
Seafood cocktail sauce, 1 tsp
Del Monte   18
Pfeiffer   25
Sour Cream
Durkee   160
French's   280
McCormick   146
Schilling   146
Soy Sauce, 1 tsp
La Choy   7
Spaghetti
Ann Page   70
  Marinara   70
  Meat   80
  Mix, 1 envelope   120
  with Mushrooms   70
Buitoni   92
  Clam, red   108
  Clam, white   144
  Marinara   88
  Meat   120

with Mushrooms	88
Durkee	45
with Mushrooms	40
French's	80
with Mushrooms	80
Franco-American	95
with Mushrooms	95
Lawry's	147
with Meatball seasoning	316
with Mushrooms	116
La Rosa	74
Prince	90
with Meat	143
with Mushrooms	103
Ragu	
Plain	96
Thick	84
Clam	88
Marinara	96
Meat	92
Thick with Meatball seasoning	104
with Mushrooms	84
Spatini	51
Town House	80
with Meat	80
with Mushrooms	89
Stroganoff	
Durkee	410
French's	165
Lawry's, 1 pkg	118

McCormick	115
Schilling	115
Sweet and Sour	
Contadina	158
Durkee	115
French's	55
La Choy	262
Swiss Steak	
Contadina	48
Taco Sauce	
Gebhardt	3
Old El Paso	4
Tartar Sauce	
Best Foods	70
Hellman's	75
Kraft	72
Lawry's	67
Seven Seas	80
Teriyaki, 1 Tbsp	
Chun King	12
French's	17
Tomato	
Contadina	45
Del Monte	40
with Bits	40
with Mushrooms	50
with Onions	50
Hunt's	35
Prima Salsa	109
Prima Salsa with Mushrooms	110

Special	40
with Bits	35
with Cheese	71
with Herbs	80
with Meat	120
with Mushrooms	40
with Onions	45
Stokely-Van Camp	35
Town House	40
Tomato Paste	
Contadina	46
Hunt's	108
Lord Mott	44
Tuna Casserole	
McCormick	128
Schilling	128
White	
Durkee	119
Wine, 1 oz	
Lawry's	
Burgundy	98
Sherry	94
White	113
Worcestershire Sauce	
Crosse & Blackwell	15
Heinz	11
French's	10
Lea & Perrins	12

Gravies, ¼ cup unless noted

Au Jus

Ann Page 1 envelope	64
Durkee	8
Durkee, Roastin' Bag, 1 pkg	64
French's	8
French's Pan Rich	30
McCormick	4
Schilling	4

Beef

Franco-American	30
Howard Johnson's	25
Wyler's	24

Brown

Ann Page 1 envelope	79
Dawn Fresh	20
Durkee	15
with Mushrooms	15
with Onions	17
Franco-American	25
French's	20
French's Pan Rich	62
McCormick	26
Herb	21
Lite	10
Pillsbury	15
Schilling	26
Herb	21

Weight Watchers 8
  with Mushrooms 12
  with Onions 13
Chicken
Ann Page, 1 envelope 120
College Inn 25
Durkee 22
  Creamy 39
  Roastin' Bag, 1 pkg 122
  Roastin' Bag Italian, 1 pkg 144
French's 25
French's Pan Rich 60
McCormick 21
  Lite 10
Pillsbury 25
Schilling 21
  Lite 10
Weight Watchers 10
Wyler's 24
Chicken Giblet
Franco-American 35
Herb
McCormick 26
Homestyle
Durkee 18
French's 25
Pillsbury 15
Meatloaf
Durkee, 1 pkg 130

Mushroom

Ann Page, 1 envelope	79
Durkee	16
Franco-American	35
French's	20
McCormick	19
Schilling	19
Wyler's	15

Mustard

French's	16

Onion

Ann Page, 1 envelope	120
Durkee	21
Durkee Roastin' Bag, 1 pkg	124
French's	25
French's Pan Rich	50

Pork

Durkee	18
Durkee Roastin' Bag, 1 pkg	130
French's	20

Pot Roast

Durkee, 1 pkg	124

Sparerib

Durkee, 1 pkg	162

Swiss Steak

Durkee	11
Durkee Roastin' Bag, 1 pkg	115

Turkey

Durkee	23

French's 25
McCormick 21
Schilling 22
Turkey Giblet
Howard Johnson's 28

CHAPTER 10

Desserts, Baking and Baked Goods

BAKING MISCELLANY

Baking Powder, 1 tsp	5
Yeast, ¼ oz unless noted	
Baker's	6
Brewer's	20
Dry, active	
Fleischmann's	20
Fresh, active	
Fleischmann's .6 oz pkg	15
Household	
Fleischmann's	7
Torula	20

10

Baking Chocolate, 1 oz

Chips

Baker's	130
Hershey's	115
Nestlé	130

Ground

Ghiradelli	150

Solid

Baker's	
German	140
semi-sweet	130
unsweetened	140
Ghiradelli	150
Hershey	190

Butterscotch

Nestlé chips	150

Coconut

Baker's	150

Ginger

Borden's crystallized	98
Borden's preserved	88

Peanut Butter

Reese chips	150

CAKES, FROZEN,
1 whole cake

Banana
Pepperidge Farm	1,115
Sara Lee	1,439

Banana Nut
Sara Lee	1,864

Black Forest
Sara Lee	1,625

Boston Creme
Pepperidge Farm	1,070

Cheesecake
Lambrecht	1,530
Mrs. Smith's	1,230
Sara Lee	
small	860
large	1,440
Cherry	1,280
French	2,190
Strawberry	1,280
Strawberry French	2,062

Chocolate
Pepperidge Farm	1,238
Sara Lee	1,380

Chocolate Bavarian
Sara Lee	2,250

10

Chocolate Fudge

Pepperidge Farm   1,800

Chocolate, German

Pepperidge Farm   1,589

Sara Lee   1,234

Coconut

Pepperidge Farm   1,800

Crumbcake

Sara Lee   170

Stouffer's

    Blueberry   211

    Chocolate Chip   225

    French   200

Cupcake

Stouffer's

    Cream   240

    Yellow   190

Devil's Food

Pepperidge Farm   1,800

Sara Lee   1,496

Golden

Pepperidge Farm   900

Sara Lee   1,440

Lemon

Sara Lee   2,175

Lemon Coconut

Pepperidge Farm   1,100

Mandarin Orange

Sara Lee   1,650

Orange
Howard Johnson's	1,700
Sara Lee	1,440

Pound
Sara Lee
Banana Nut	1,170
Chocolate	1,220
Chocolate Swirl	1,300
Plain	1,320
Raisin	1,270

Pepperidge Farm
Apple Nut	1,300
Butter	1,300
Carrot	1,600
Chocolate	1,300

Cherry
Mrs. Smith's	2,335

Strawberry
Mrs. Smith's	1,830
Sara Lee	1,550
Strawberry and Cream	1,700

Vanilla
Pepperidge Farm	1,900

Walnut
Sara Lee	1,690

CAKE MIXES, 1 whole cake

Angel Food
Betty Crocker	1,560
One Step	1,680
Confetti	1,800
Strawberry	1,800
Duncan Hines	1,670
Pillsbury	1,680
Swans Down	1,590

Apple Raisin
Duncan Hines	2,280
Spicy	1,620

Applesauce Raisin
Betty Crocker	1,800

Banana
Betty Crocker	3,140
Duncan Hines	2,400
Pillsbury	3,120

Banana Nut
Betty Crocker	1,800
Duncan Hines	1,800

Bundt
Pillsbury
Fudge	3,480
Lemon	3,350
Macaroon	3,950
Marble	3,960

Pound	3,710
Triple Fudge	3,590
Butter	
Duncan Hines	3,240
Pillsbury	2,680
Butter Brickle	
Betty Crocker	3,110
Butter Fudge	
Duncan Hines	3,240
Butter Pecan	
Betty Crocker	3,120
Cheesecake	
Jello-O	2,000
Pillsbury	3,120
Royal	1,840
Cherry	
Duncan Hines	2,280
Cherry Chip	
Betty Crocker	2,280
Chocolate	
Betty Crocker	1,380
Duncan Hines	2,400
Pillsbury Dark	3,120
Swans Down	2,240
Chocolate Almond	
Betty Crocker	1,890
Chocolate Chip	
Betty Crocker	1,980
Duncan Hines	1,710
Double Chocolate Chip	1,620

Chocolate Fudge
Betty Crocker	3,240

Chocolate, German
Betty Crocker	3,240
Pillsbury	3,120

Chocolate, Sour Cream
Betty Crocker	3,240
Duncan Hines	2,400

Chocolate, Swiss
Duncan Hines	2,400
Swans Down	2,240

Chocolate with frosting
Betty Crocker	1,620

Coconut Pecan
Betty Crocker	1,975

Date Nut
Betty Crocker	1,890

Devil's Food
Betty Crocker	3,240
Duncan Hines	2,400
Pillsbury	3,240
Swans Down	2,230

Fudge Marble
Duncan Hines	2,400
Pillsbury	3,240

Gingerbread
Betty Crocker	1,890

Lemon
Betty Crocker	3,240
Pudding Cake	1,380

10

Duncan Hines	2,400
Pillsbury	3,240

Lemon Chiffon
Betty Crocker	2,280

Marble
Betty Crocker	3,280

Orange
Betty Crocker	3,240
Duncan Hines	2,400

Pineapple
Betty Crocker	2,400
Duncan Hines	2,400

Pound
Betty Crocker	2,280

Spice
Betty Crocker	3,240
Duncan Hines	2,400

Spice Raisin
Betty Crocker	1,800

Strawberry
Betty Crocker	3,240
Duncan Hines	2,400

Streusel
Pillsbury
Cinnamon	4,080
Devil's Food	3,950
Fudge Marble	4,080
Chocolate	3,950
Lemon	4,200

10

White

Betty Crocker	2,400
Duncan Hines	2,280
Pillsbury	3,000
Swans Down	2,120

Yellow

Betty Crocker	3,240
Butter	2,880
with frosting	1,380
Duncan Hines	2,400
Pillsbury	3,120
Swans Down	2,240

CAKES FOR SNACKS, 1 cake

Big Wheels	170
Brownie	
Hostess	
small	150
large	240
Chocolate, cream-filled	
Yankee Doodles	134
Choco-Diles	250
Creamies, 1 pkg	
Tastykake	
Chocolate	255

Spice	270
Crumb Cakes	
Hostess	130
Cupcakes	
Hostess	
Chocolate	155
Orange	147
Tastykake, 1 pkg	
Buttercream	238
Chocolate	200
Chocolate Cream	239
Devil Dogs	169
Devil's Food	
Hostess	140
Drake's	135
Ding Dongs	170
Donuts	
Hostess	
Cinnamon	110
Crunch	100
Enrobed	130
Plain	105
Powdered	115
Funny Bones, 1 pkg	162
Ho-Ho's	120
Juniors, 1 pkg	
Tastykake	
Chocolate	307
Coconut	330
Coffee cake	310

Krimpets, 1 pkg
   Tastykake
      Butterscotch   190
      Chocolate   255
      Jelly   168
      Vanilla   240
Macaroons
   Hostess   210
Oatmeal Raisin, 1 pkg
   Tastykake   267
Orange Treats, 1 pkg
   Tastykake   230
Pound
   Drake's
      Marble   185
      Plain   181
      Raisin   323
Ring Ding   366
Sno Balls   140
Tandy Takes, 1 pkg
      Chocolate   180
      Peanut Butter   190
Teens, 1 pkg   225
Tempty, 1 pkg
      Chocolate   196
      Lemon   259
Tiger Tails   415
Twinkies   140

COFFEE CAKE, 1 cake

Almond
  Sara Lee   1,350
  Sara Lee Coffee Ring   1,100
Angel Food
  Howard Johnson's   710
Apple
  Morton   1,130
  Sara Lee   1,175
Apple Cinnamon
  Pillsbury   1,880
Apricot
  Sara Lee   1,176
Banana
  Sara Lee   1,440
Blueberry
  Sara Lee Coffee Ring   1,080
  Sara Lee Danish   1,175
Butter Pecan
  Pillsbury   2,480
Butter Streusel
  Sara Lee   1,395
Cherry
  Sara Lee   1,050
Chocolate
  Sara Lee   1,375

10

Chocolate, German

Morton	1,360
Sara Lee	1,230

Cinnamon Streusel

Pillsbury	2,000
Sara Lee	1,230

Coconut

Pepperidge Farm	1,940

Coffee Cake

Aunt Jemima	1,360

Crumb

Drake's	1,460

Lemon

Drake's	1,030

Maple Crunch

Sara Lee	1,157

Orange

Sara Lee	1,442

Pecan

Drake's	1,109
Morton	1,368
Sara Lee small	764
Sara Lee large	1,320

Raspberry

Sara Lee	1,090

Sour Cream

Pillsbury	2,160

COOKIES, 1 piece

Adelaide
  Pepperidge Farm   53
Almond
  Keebler   47
  Stella D'Oro   49
Almond Spice
  Keebler   50
Angel Puffs
  Stella D'Oro   17
Animal Crackers
  Keebler   12
  Nabisco   12
  Sunshine   10
Animal Crackers Iced
  Keebler   52
  Sunshine   26
Anise
  Stella D'Oro
    Anisette Sponge   50
    Anisette Toast   34
Apple
  Keebler   27
  Nabisco   48
Applesauce
  Sunshine   33
    Iced   104

Arrowroot
Nabisco   22
Sunshine   16

Assorted
Stella D'Oro
  Hostess   39
  Lady Stella   37

Bordeaux
Pepperidge Farm   37

Breakfast Treats
Stella D'Oro   100

Brown Edge
Nabisco   28

Brown Sugar
Nabisco   25
Pepperidge Farm   50

Brussels
Pepperidge Farm   57

Butter
Keebler   84
Nabisco   37
Pepperidge Farm   38
Sunshine   24

Capri
Pepperidge Farm   85

Cashew
Nabisco   57

Chessman
Pepperidge Farm   43

Chocolate Chip Coconut
Keebler 80
Nabisco 76
Sunshine 76

Chocolate Strawberry Wafers
Estee 90

Cinnamon
Sunshine 20

Cinnamon Almond
Nabisco 53

Cinnamon Sugar
Fun Days 48
Pepperidge Farm 52

Coconut
Keebler 61
  Old Fashioned 83
  Strip 37
Nabisco 16
Stella D'Oro 47
Sunshine 47

Coconut, Iced
Keebler Crunchies 70

Coconut Chocolate
Pepperidge Farm 83

Creme Sandwiches
Butterscotch
  Keebler 85
Chocolate
  Keebler Dutch 95

Keebler Opera	85
Oreo grocery	50
Oreo individual	40
Chocolate fudge	
Cookie Mates	53
Keebler	97
Sunshine	74
Coconut	
Nabisco	53
Sunshine	51
Wise Coco	39
Lemon	
Keebler	85
Swiss	
Nabisco	43
Vanilla	
Cameo	68
Cookie Mates	52
Keebler	82
French	95
Opera	85
Sunshine	79
Vienna Fingers	69
Wise	38
Crescents	
Nabisco	34
Cup Custard	
Sunshine	70
Danish Wedding	
Keebler	31

Date Nut
Pepperidge Farm 53
Sunshine 82

Devil's Food
Keebler 64
Nabisco 58
Sunshine 55

Dixie Vanilla
Sunshine 60

Egg Biscuits
Stella D'Oro 37
   Anise 135
   Egg Jumbo 43
   Rum and Brandy 135
   Sugared 135
   Vanilla 130

Figs
Nabisco Fig Newtons 59
Frito-Lay 189
Keebler 71
Sunshine 42

Fruit
Stella D'Oro 67
Sunshine Golden Fruit 61

Fruit, Iced
Nabisco 70

Fudge
Keebler
   Sticks 42

Strips	57
Pepperidge Farm	58
Gingerbread	
Pepperidge Farm	33
Gingerbread, Iced	
Keebler	130
Ginger Snaps	
Keebler	39
Nabisco	30
Sunshine	
small	14
large	32
Golden Bars	
Stella D'Oro	110
Graham Crackers	
Keebler	
Honey	17
Thin	17
Very Thin	14
Nabisco	30
Honey Maid	30
Sunshine	17
Sugar Honey	30
Graham Crackers, chocolate covered	
Keebler	44
Milco	91
Nabisco	55
Fancy Dip	68
Pantry	62
Robena	72

Kichel
Stella D'Oro   64
Lady Joan
Sunshine   42
Sunshine Iced   47
LaLanne
Sunshine   15
Lemon
Keebler   83
Nabisco   17
Sunshine   76
   Lemon Coolers   29
Lemon Nut
Pepperidge Farm   58
Lido
Pepperidge Farm   95
Love Cookies
Stella D'Oro   110
Macaroons
Sunshine   85
   Butter   39
   Coconut   81
Bake Shop   87
Nabisco   71
Mandel Toast
Stella D'Oro   54
Margherite
Stella D'Oro   73
Marigold Sandwich
Keebler   91

Marshmallow
Chocolate covered
Keebler

Dainties	68
Galaxies	82
Treasures	83
Tulips	83

Coconut

Nabisco	54
Sunshine	70

Iced
Sunshine

Frosted Cakes	68
Nut Sundae	74

Mallomars	60

Nabisco

Puffs	94
Twirls	133
Pinwheels	139

Sunshine

Puffs	63
Kings	135

Sandwich

Keebler	81
Nabisco	32

Sprinkles

Sunshine	71

Milano

Pepperidge Farm	63
Mint	70

Molasses Crisps
Pepperidge Farm   30
Molasses and Spice
Sunshine   67
Nassau
Pepperidge Farm   75
Oatmeal
Keebler   78
Nabisco
   Family Favorite   24
   Home Style   60
Sunshine   63
Oatmeal Almond
Pepperidge Farm   53
Oatmeal, Iced
Keebler   82
Oatmeal Marmalade
Pepperidge Farm   53
Oatmeal Peanut Butter
Sunshine   79
Oatmeal Raisin
Bake Shop   76
Nabisco   77
Pepperidge Farm   54
Orleans
Pepperidge Farm   33
Peanut
Pepperidge Farm   47
Sunshine   33

Peanut Butter
  Keebler 81
  Nabisco Nutter Butter 69
  Sunshine
    Crunch 68
    Patties 30
Peanut Butter, Chocolate-covered
  Eton 53
  Keebler 117
Peanut Caramel
  Hey Days 122
Peanut Cream
  Nabisco 34
Pecan
  Keebler 20
  Sunshine 78
Pfeffernusse
  Stella D'Oro 44
Pirouette
  Pepperidge Farm 40
Prune
  Stella D'Oro 87
Raisin
  Nabisco 56
  Stella D'Oro 115
  Sunshine 73
Raisin, Iced
  Keebler 81

10

Raisin Bran
Pepperidge Farm   53

Shortbread
Keebler   27
Lorna Doone   38
Pepperidge Farm   65
Scottie   39

Shortbread with Cashews
Nabisco   50

Shortbread, Chocolate-covered
Nabisco   50

Shortbread with Coconut   65
Shortbread, Iced   58
Shortbread Pecans
Keebler   77
Nabisco   77

St. Moritz
Pepperidge Farm   47

Sorrento
Stella D'Oro   57

Sprinkles
Sunshine   57

Sugar
Eton   50
Keebler
    Giant   70
    Old Fashioned   81
Nabisco   17
Pepperidge Farm   53

Sugar Wafers
  Nabisco Biscos 18
    Creme Waffles 47
  Keebler 26
  Kreemlined 45
  Regent 23
  Sunshine 47

Sugar Wafers, Chocolate-covered
  Eton 54
  Milco 80
  Nabisco 76
    Creme Stix 50
  Sunshine 30

Sugar Wafers, Spiced
  Nabisco 33

Sunflower Raisin
  Pepperidge Farm 53

Swedish Creme 103

Swiss Chalet 97

Swiss Fudge
  Stella D'Oro 64

Tahiti
  Pepperidge Farm 85

Taste of Vienna
  Stella D'Oro 85

Tea Biscuits
  Nabisco 21

Toy Cookies
  Sunshine 13

Vanilla
  Keebler   19
  Nabisco
    Snaps   13
    Wafers   18
  Sunshine   15
Vanilla Thins
  Estee   25
Vienna Finger Sandwich
  Sunshine   71
Yum Yums
  Sunshine   83
Zanzibar
  Pepperidge Farm   37

PASTRY, FROZEN, MIXES, AND TOASTER, 1 piece unless noted

Dessert mixes
  Pillsbury Appleasy   160
Donuts
  Morton
    Bavarian Creme   180
    Boston Creme   205

Chocolate	150
Glazed	150
Jelly	180
Mini	120
Town House Cinnamon	210

Dumplings, apple
Pepperidge Farm	280

Strudel, apple
Pepperidge Farm, 1 oz	85

Tarts
Kellogg's Pop Tarts	210
Pepperidge Farm	
Apple	280
Blueberry	285
Cherry	280
Lemon	310
Raspberry	320

Popovers (Flako) — 166

Turnovers
Pepperidge Farm	320
Pillsbury	180

PIES, FROZEN, 1 whole pie

Apple
Banquet	1,440

10

Morton	1,740
Mini	590
Mrs. Smith's	1,768
Natural	2,881
Dutch	1,860
Tart	1,495

Banana Cream
Banquet	1,032
Morton	1,020
Mini	230
Mrs. Smith's	1,290
Light	1,320

Blueberry
Banquet	1,523
Morton	1,680
Mini	580
Mrs. Smith's	1,740
Natural	2,040

Boston Cream
Mrs. Smith's	1,980

Cherry
Banquet	1,360
Morton	1,805
Mini	591
Mrs. Smith's	1,860
Natural	2,040

Chocolate
Mrs. Smith's	1,500
Royal Dutch	2,040

Chocolate Cream
Banquet   1,060
Morton   1,200
  Mini   260
Mrs. Smith's   1,470
Coconut
Mrs. Smith's   1,380
Coconut Cream
Banquet   1,040
Morton   1,140
  Mini   260
Mrs. Smith's   1,380
Coconut Custard
Banquet   1,220
Morton
  Mini   370
Mrs. Smith's   1,590
Custard
Banquet   1,240
Devil Cream
Royal   2,280
Mrs. Smith's   1,470
Lemon
Mrs. Smith's   2,040
Royal   2,080
Lemon Cream
Banquet   1,000
Morton   1,000
  Mini   240
Mrs. Smith's   1,350

Lemon Crunch
  Mrs. Smith's   2,480
Lemon Meringue
  Mrs. Smith's   1,560
Lemon Yogurt
  Mrs. Smith's   1,200
Mince
  Morton   1,860
    Mini   590
  Mrs. Smith's   2,010
Mincemeat
  Banquet   1,520
Neapolitan Cream
  Morton   1,140
  Mrs. Smith's   1,440
Nesselrode
  Royal   2,000
Peach
  Banquet   1,320
  Morton   1,680
    Mini   560
  Mrs. Smith's   1,800
    Natural   1,980
Pecan
  Morton
    Mini   580
  Mrs. Smith's   2,589
Pineapple
  Mrs. Smith's   1,800

Pineapple-Cheese
 Mrs. Smith's   1,580
Pumpkin
 Banquet   1,230
 Morton   1,380
  Mini   430
 Mrs. Smith's   1,440
Raisin
 Mrs. Smith's   1,890
Spumoni
 Royal   2,120
Strawberry Cream
 Banquet   1,020
 Morton   1,080
 Mrs. Smith's   1,320
Strawberry and Rhubarb
 Mrs. Smith's   1,890
  Natural   1,920
Strawberry-Yogurt
 Mrs. Smith's   1,220

Pie Mixes, 1 whole pie

Betty Crocker Boston Cream   2,080
Pillsbury
 Chocolate Cream   2,460
 Lemon Chiffon   1,980
 Vanilla   2,340

Pie Crusts and Shells, 1 piece

Pastry Sheets
  Pepperidge Farm   570
Pastry Shells
  Pepperidge Farm   240
  Stella D'Oro   146
Pie Crusts
  Betty Crocker   1,920
    Stick   960
  Flako   1,560
  Pillsbury   1,740
Pie Shells
  Pepperidge Farm   521
    shallow   440
    with top   760
  Stella D'Oro   240
Tart Shells
  Pepperidge Farm   88

Pie Fillings, 1 whole can unless noted

Apple
  Wilderness   660
Apricot
  Wilderness   720
Banana Cream
  Jell-O   660

Blueberry
Wilderness 660
Cherry
Wilderness 650
Lemon
Jell-O 1,080
Royal, 1 cup 310
Wilderness 840
Lime
Royal, 1 cup 310
Mince
Wilderness 840
Mincemeat
None Such, 1 cup 660
Peach
Wilderness 655
Pumpkin
Libby's, 1 cup 205
Stokely-Van Camp, 1 cup 370
Raisin
Wilderness 720
Strawberry
Wilderness 710

SMALL PASTRY PIES, 1 piece

Apple
Stella D'Oro	90
Hostess	400
Tastykake	350
Tastykake French	400

Blueberry
Hostess	365

Cherry
Hostess	420
Tastykake	380

Fig
Stella D'Oro	100

Guava
Stella D'Oro	125

Lemon
Hostess	420
Tastykake	355

Peach/Apricot
Stella D'Oro	90

Pecan
Frito-Lay	345

Prune
Stella D'Oro	92

Puff Pastry
Durkee	
Beef	47

Cheese	59
Chicken	49
Chicken liver	48
Shrimp	44

PUDDINGS, MIXES AND CANNED, ½ cup, unless noted

Banana
Ann Page	250
Del Monte	180
Shak-A-Pudd'n	165
Royal	164

Banana Cream
| *Jell-O* | 175 |
| *My-T-Fine* | 175 |

Bavarian Cream
| *My-T-Fine* | 176 |

Butter Pecan
| *My-T-Fine* | 175 |

Butterscotch
Ann Page	190
Instant	170
Del Monte	175

D-Zerta	25
Foremost	175
Jell-O	172
My-T-Fine	170
Royal	190
Sego	250
Caramel Nut	
Royal	195
Cherry	
Whip 'n Chill	139
Cherry-Plum	
Junket	135
Chocolate	
Ann Page	180
Betty Crocker	180
Bounty	174
Dannon	150
Del Monte	250
D-Zerta	20
Foremost	175
Jell-O	175
Instant	190
My-T-Fine	185
Royal	190
Dark 'N Sweet	200
Sego	250
Shak-A-Pudd'n	200
Whip 'n Chill	145
Chocolate Almond	
My-T-Fine	196

Chocolate Fudge
  Betty Crocker 180
  Del Monte 190
  Foremost 175
  Jell-O 175
    Instant 191
  My-T-Fine 190
  Sego 250
  Whip 'n Chill 139
Chocolate Malt
  Shak-A-Pudd'n 200
Chocolate Marshmallow
  Sego 250
Coconut
  Ann Page
    Cream 190
    Toasted 170
  Jell-O 175
    Instant 190
  Royal 185
Currant-Raspberry
  Junket 135
Custard
  Ann Page 150
  Jell-O 165
  My-T-Fine
    Caramel 145
    Vanilla 156
  Rice-A-Roni 120
  Royal 145

Indian
B & M	150

Lemon
Ann Page	150
Instant	180
Bounty	196
Foremost	197
Jell-O	178
Instant	179
My-T-Fine	180
Royal	180
Whip 'n Chill	135

Lemon Chiffon
Jell-O	144

Mocha Nut
Royal	190

Pineapple Cream
Jell-O	165
Instant	179

Pistachio
Ann Page	180
Royal	180

Plum
Crosse & Blackwell	255
R & R	300

Rice
Betty Crocker	150
Bounty	195

Strawberry
Junket	135

10

Sego	250
Shak-A-Pudd'n	165
Whip 'n Chill	135

CHAPTER 11

Jellies, Syrups, Toppings and Spreads

DESSERT TOPPINGS, 1 Tbsp

Black Cherry
  No-Cal   0
Black Raspberry
  No-Cal   0
Butterscotch
  Hershey's   55
  Kraft   60
  Smucker's   69
Caramel
  Kraft
    chocolate   56

vanilla	57
Smucker's	69
peanut butter	75
Cherry	
Smucker's	65
Chocolate	
Bosco	50
Hershey's	45
Kraft	50
No-Cal	6
Smucker's	65
Tillie Lewis	16
Chocolate Fudge	
Hershey's	45
Kraft	70
Smucker's	65
Swiss	72
Chocolate Mint	
Hershey's	61
Smucker's	67
Chocolate Peanut Butter	
Hershey's	60
Coffee	
No-Cal	6
Cola	
No-Cal	0
Cream, whipped	
Reddi-Whip	8
Top-Whip	7

Grape
  No-Cal — 0
Hard Sauce
  Crosse & Blackwell — 64
Marshmallow
  Kraft — 35
Pecans in Syrup
  Kraft — 82
  Smucker's — 65
Pineapple
  Kraft — 50
  Smucker's — 62
Strawberry
  Kraft — 45
  No-Cal — 0
  Smucker's — 60
Walnut
  Kraft — 88
Walnuts in Syrup
  Smucker's — 65
Whip, non-dairy
  Cool Whip — 14
  D-Zerta — 8
  Dream Whip — 10
  Kraft — 9
  Lucky Whip — 11
  Pet — 16
  Reddi-Whip — 9

FROSTINGS, 1 can

Betty Crocker
Chocolate Fudge	1920
Coconut Pecan	1310
White, creamy	1920
White, fluffy *Lite*	720
All other flavors	1800

Pillsbury
Coconut Pecan	1800
White, fluffy	840
All other flavors	2040

GELATIN, ½ cup

Borden's
Cherry	80
Fruit Cocktail	109
Mandarin Orange	89
Perfection	81
Pineapple-papaya	78
Pineapple-raspberry	77
Strawberry	75

Jell-O

1-2-3	81
Best	77

Knox unflavored, dry, 1 envelope   28

Royal   80

JELLIES AND BUTTERS, 1 Tbsp

Apple Butter

Bama	31
Smucker's	
Cider	39
Spiced	39
Peach	45
Ma Brown	32
Musselman's	33

Jams

Ann Page	51
Bama	51
Diet Delight	22
Kraft	49
S & W	10
Smucker's	54
Slenderella	24
artificially sweetened	1

11

Jellies

Ann Page	54
Bama	51
Crosse & Blackwell	51
Diet Delight	21
Home Brands	54
Kraft	48
Low Calorie	22
Ma Brown	49
Musselman's	53
S & W	12
Smucker's	51
Slenderella	24
Single Service	50
Welch's	50

Marmalade

Ann Page	54
Bama	54
Kraft	54
Low Calorie	25
S & W	11
Smucker's	49
Slenderella	24

Preserves

Ann Page	54
Bama	51
Crosse & Blackwell	59
Empress	54
Home Brands	54
Kraft	48

Low Calorie	25
Regular	55
Ma Brown	51
S & W	11
Smucker's	54
Welch's	54
Spreads	
Smucker's	24
Tillie Lewis	12

SPREADS, 1 Tbsp

Anchovy Paste	
Crosse & Blackwell	20
Chicken	
Swanson	35
Underwood	32
Chicken Salad	
Carnation	31
Corned Beef	
Underwood	28
Ham	
Carnation	26
Hormel	35
Libby's	100
Underwood	48

11

Liverwurst
  Underwood   46
Peanut Butter
  Ann Page   105
  Bama   100
    and jelly   82
  Datetree   93
  Home Brands   100
  Jif   93
  Kitchen King   95
  Peter Pan   94
  Planters   95
  Roberts   93
  Skippy   95
  Smucker's   95
    Goober Grape   63
  Sultana   101
Potted Meat
  Libby's   140
Roast Beef
  Underwood   29
Sandwich Spread
  Best Foods   60
  Hellman's   58
  Mrs. Filbert's   53
  Nu Made   51
  Oscar Mayer   33
Spam
  Hormel   40

Tuna
  Carnation   26
Turkey Salad
  Carnation   27

SUGAR, SYRUPS, SWEETENERS AND HONEY

Honey, 1 Tbsp	64
1 cup	1,031
Sugar, 1 cup	
Brown	
loosely packed	540
firmly packed	820
Maple	790
Powdered	460
sifted	385
White, granulated	770
1 Tbsp	45
Sweeteners, Sugar Substitutes	
Dia-Mel Sugar-Like, 1 gram pkt	3
Dia-Mel Sweet'n-it Liquid	0
Featherweight Sug'r Like, 1 tsp	2
Pillsbury Sprinkle Sweet, 1 tsp	2

Pillsbury Sweet 10	0
Sweet'n Low, 1 gram pkt	3½
Weight Watchers Sweet'ner, 1 gram pkt	3
Whitlock Suprose, 1 gram pkt	4

Syrup, 1 Tbsp

Aunt Jemima	53
Cary's Diet	10
Cary's Maple	60
Diet Delight	15
Golden Griddle	50
Karo	60
Corn	58
Maple	54
Log Cabin	
Buttered	52
Country Kitchen	53
Maple	46
Maple-Honey	55
Mrs. Butterworth's	54
S & W	12
Tillie Lewis	14
Molasses	
dark	45
light	50
Sorghum	55

CHAPTER 12

Candies, Ice Cream and Nuts

CANDY, 1 oz

Jellied Candy

Dots	100
Jujubes	50
Jujyfruits	94
Mason	99
Quaker City	93
Red Hot Dollars	94

Licorice

Black Crows	101
Diamond Drops	98
Good & Plenty	99
Heide Pastilles	96
Switzer	97

Lifesavers, 1 piece	7

Malted Milk

Walter Johnson	131
Mars	126

Marshmallows

Campfire	100
Curtiss	97
Kraft	96
Jet Puff	125
Macaroon	110
Milky Way	119

Mints

Kraft	105
Richardson	110

Mints, chocolate-coated

Mason	203

Nestlé's	121
Welch's	108
Nougat	
Bit-O-Honey	116
Bit-O-Peanut Butter	118
Nougat, nuts and chocolate	
Oh Henry	131
Powerhouse	122
Nut Brittle	
Bonomo	115
Kraft	120
Chocolate-coated	130
Planters Cashew	135
Peanut	139
Nuts, chocolate-coated	
Hershey	
Almonds	143
Peanuts	140
Kraft	
Almonds	155
Brazil nuts	166
Peanuts	152
Welch's peanuts	157
Nuts and Caramel, chocolate-coated	
Choc-O-Nuts	132
Kraft	
Almond	155
Cashew	153
Peanut	151

Laddie Bar	133
Old Nick	134
Welch's	124
Peanut Butter, chocolate-coated	
Reese	148
Popcorn, caramel-coated	
Cracker Jack	132
King Korn	117
Old London	117
Wise	103
Raisins, chocolate-coated	
Kraft	115
Welch's	102
Snickers	128
Taffy	
Bonomo Turkish	104
Williamson Kisses	125
Toffee	
Kraft	112
chocolate-covered with almond	144
Tootsie Pops	149
Tootsie Roll	115
Trident Mints	8
Triple Decker	148

GUM, 1 piece

Adams	9
Beeman	10
Beech-Nut	9
Beechies	6
Black Jack	9
Bubble Yum	25
Bubblicious	24
Care Free	8
Chiclets	6
Clorets	6
Clove	5
Dentyne	5
Estee	3
Freshen-Up	9
Fruit Stripe	9
Orbit	8
Trident	5
Wrigley's	10

ICE CREAM, 1 cup (½ pint)

Black Raspberry
   Breyer's   264
Black Walnut
   Meadow Gold   329
Butter Almond
   Sealtest   326
Butter Almond and Chocolate
   Breyer's   318
Butter Brickle
   Sealtest   299
Butter Pecan
   Meadow Gold   300
   Sealtest   322
Butterscotch Pecan
   Breyer's   302
Caramel Pecan
   Breyer's   320
Cherry
   Sealtest   276
Cherry-Vanilla
   Breyer's   280
   Meadow Gold   280
   Sealtest   265
Chocolate
   Borden's   255
   Breyer's   314

Carnation	253
Howard Johnson's	519
Meadow Gold	278
Sealtest	281
Swift's	257
Chocolate Almond	
Breyer's	366
Dutch	299
Sealtest	324
Chocolate Chip	
Breyer's Mint	344
Meadow Gold	295
Sealtest	291
Coconut	
Sealtest	321
Coffee	
Breyer's	287
Sealtest	288
Lemon	
Sealtest	272
Maple Walnut	
Sealtest	322
Peach	
Meadow Gold	259
Sealtest	253
Pineapple	
Sealtest	251
Strawberry	
Bordens	253
Breyer's	253

Howard Johnson's	414
Meadow Gold	281
Sealtest	254
Swift's	242
Vanilla	
Bordens	246
Breyer's	299
Carnation	250
Howard Johnson's	500
Meadow Gold	280
Sealtest	289
Swift's	267
Sealtest	280
Vanilla-Fudge	
Breyer's	300
Vanilla-Raspberry	
Sealtest	279

Ice Milk, 1 cup	200

Sherbet, 1 cup	260

Ice Cream Bars, 1

Bi-sicle	110
Creamsicle	78
Dreamsicle	70
Dreamstick	180
Drumstick	183
Fudgesicle	100
Good Humor	
Almond	218
Chocolate	222
Ice	50
Chocolate-covered vanilla	169
Whammy	105
Popsicle	72
Sealtest	
Orange Cream	71
Orange Treat	89

Ice Cream Cones and Cups, 1 item

Comet	
cone	19
cone, rolled sugar	35
cup	20

12

Take-Out Ice Cream, 1 item

Baskin Robbins

Banana Daiquiri Ice	129
Butter Pecan	195
Chocolate Fudge	229
Chocolate Mint	189
Jamoca	182
Mango Sherbert	132
Peach	165
Rocky Road	205
Strawberry	168
Vanilla	217

Bridgeman's

Plain cone	170
Sugar cone	200

Dairy Queen

Banana Split	540
Cone	
large	340
medium	230
small	110
Float	330
Freeze	520
Malt	
large	840
medium	600
small	340
Parfait	460
Sandwich	140

Sundae	
large	400
medium	300
small	170
Friendly's	
Fribble	
chocolate	470
vanilla	420
Sundae	
vanilla fudge	420
vanilla strawberry	340

NUTS AND SEEDS, 1 oz

Almonds	
Blue Diamond	179
Franklin	154
Granny Goose	155
Planters	170
Cashews	
A & P	170
Frito-Lay	170
Franklin	145
Granny Goose	170
Planters	170
Skippy	163

12

Filberts

Franklin	164

Mixed

A & P	190
Excel	190
Franklin	160
with peanuts	156
Granny Goose	168
Planters	180
with peanuts	185
Skippy	172

Peanuts

A & P	180
in shell	170
Excel	180
Frito-Lay	175
in shell	160
Spanish	170
Granny Goose	168
Planters	170
Spanish, dry roasted	162
Peanut Crisps	150
Skippy	165
Tavern Nuts	171

Pecans

A & P	200
Granny Goose	203
Planters	190

Pistachios

Frito-Lay	174

Granny Goose	176
Planters	169
Sesame Mix	
Planters	163
Soybeans	
Malt-O-Meal	
dry roasted	132
oil roasted	141
Planters	133
Sunflower Seeds	
whole, 1 lb	1,371
whole, 1 cup	257
hulled, 1 cup	810

CHAPTER 13

Fast Foods and Snacks

CHIPS, PUFFS, CRISPS, ETC.
1 oz unless noted

13

Salted	121
Sesame	119
Whole wheat	122
Taco Chips	
Old London	127
Tortilla Chips	
Doritos	
Nachos	137
Tacos	142
Granny Goose	144
Planters	
Nachos	128
Tacos	132
Wheat Chips	
Bakon Snacks	147

PIZZA, FROZEN, 1 whole
pizza unless noted

Beef and Cheese	
El Chico	
with enchilada	1,010
with taco	990
Bacon	
Tostino's	704

Cheese
Buitoni 276
Celeste 473
  large 1,280
  Sicilian 1,395
  with mushroom, small 459
  with mushroom, large 1,205
Chef Boy-Ar-Dee 798
  small 160
Jeno's 840
  Deluxe 1,470
  Junior 165
  Mix 838
Kraft 822
  Pee Wee 170
Lambrecht 909
La Pizzeria 1,230
Lean Cuisine 170
Roman 891
Stouffer's 330
Tostino's 882

Cheese and Refried Beans
El Chico 902

Cheese and Chili
El Chico 1,039

Combinations
Celeste 600
  large 1,480
Jeno's Deluxe 1,667

La Pizzeria	830
large	1,529
Stouffer's	789
Tostino's	1,683
Classic	1,675

Hamburger

Jeno's	888
Tostino's	910
Crisp	955

Open Face

Buitoni	250

Pepperoni

Celeste	540
large	1,438
Chef Boy-Ar-Dee	175
Jeno's	901
La Pizzeria	1,322
Roman	889
Stouffer's	800
Tostino's	923
Crisp	960
Classic	1,792
Classic with mushrooms	1,497

Rolls

Jeno's	
Cheeseburger	268
Pepperoni	262
Sausage	259
Shrimp	214

Sausage

Celeste	561
large	1,500
Jeno's	899
Deluxe	1,495
Mix	1,058
Kraft	1,000
Pee Wee	190
Lambrecht	1,005
La Pizzeria	860
large	1,515
Roman	233
Tostino's	938
Crisp	981
Classic	1,799

POPCORN AND PRETZELS

Popcorn, 1 cup

Jiffy Pop	31
Jolly Time	31
King Korn	
Cheese	40
Seasoned	42
Pops-Rite	38

Presto-Pop	37
3 Minute	38
TNT	52
Wise	43
Cheese-flavored	49
Wonder	45
Pretzels, 1 piece	
Bachman	
B's	8
Beer	55
Medium	20
Teeny	11
Thin	18
Old London	5
Nabisco Mister Salty	
Dutch	51
3-Ring	12
Veri-Thin	20
Pretzelettes	6
Sunshine	19

FAST FOODS

Arby's	
Beef and Cheese Sandwich	450
Club Sandwich	560

Ham and Cheese Sandwich	380
Junior Roast Beef Sandwich	220
Roast Beef Sandwich	350
Super Roast Beef Sandwich	620
Swiss King Sandwich	660
Turkey Deluxe Sandwich	510
Turkey Sandwich	410

Arthur Treacher's

Chicken	271
Chicken Sandwich	265
Chips	243
Chowder	66
Cole Slaw	144
Fish	241
Fish Sandwich	282
Krunch Pup	358
Lemon Luvs	324
Shrimp	380

Brazier (Dairy Queen)

Hamburger	260
Cheeseburger	320
Big Brazier	460
Big Brazier with Cheese	550
Big Brazier with Lettuce and Tomato	470
Super Brazier (The Half-Pounder)	780
Hot Dog	270
Hot Dog with Chili	330
Hot Dog with Cheese	330
Fish Sandwich	400
Fish Sandwich with Cheese	440

French Fries	200
French Fries, large	320
Onion Rings	300

Burger Chef

Chocolate Shake	310
Big Chef	542
Cheeseburger	304
Double Cheeseburger	434
Double Hamburger	325
French Fries	187
Hamburger	258
Mariner Platter	680
Rancher Platter	640
Shake	326
Skipper's Treat	604
Super Chef	600

Burger King

Whopper	650
Double Beef *Whopper*	850
Whopper with Cheese	760
Double Beef *Whopper* with Cheese	970
Whopper Junior	360
Whopper Junior with Cheese	420
Whopper Junior with Double Meat	490
Whopper Junior Double Meat with Cheese	550
Hamburger	310
Hamburger with Cheese	360
Double Meat Hamburger	440
Double Meat Hamburger with Cheese	540

Steak Sandwich	600
Whaler	660
Whaler with Cheese	770
Onion Rings, large	330
Onion Rings, regular	230
French Fries, large bag	360
French Fries, regular bag	240
Chocolate Milkshake	380
Vanilla Milkshake	360
Apple Pie	240

Carl's Jr.

Famous Star Hamburger	480
Super Star Hamburger	660
Old Time Star Hamburger	440
Happy Star Hamburger	290
Steak Sandwich	630
California Roast Beef Sandwich	380
Fish Fillet Sandwich	550
Original Hot Dog	340
Chili Dog	360
Chili Cheese Dog	400
American Cheese	40
Salad with Condiments 11 oz	170
Dressing, 2 oz	
Blue Cheese	200
Thousand Island	190
Lo-Cal Italian	48
French Fries	220
Apple Turnover	330

Carrot Cake	380
Shake	310
Soft Drinks	200

***Church's Fried Chicken*, 1 piece, boned**

Dark	305
White	327

Dunkin' Donuts

Cake and Chocolate Cake Donuts	
rings, sticks, crullers, etc.	240
Yeast-raised Donuts	160
Glazed Yeast-Raised Donuts	168
Fancies	
coffee rolls, danish, etc.	215
Fancies with Filling and Topping	260
Munchkins, Yeast-raised	26
Munchkins, Cake and Chocolate Cake	66
Munchkins with Filling and Topping	79

Gino's

Apple Pie	238
Cheeseburger	300
Cheese Hero	738
Cheese Sirloiner	532
Coke	117
Fish Platter	650
Fish Sandwich	450
French Fries	156
Giant	569
Hamburger	254
Hero	647
Hot Chocolate	90

Hardees

Apple Turnover	282
Big Twin	447
Cheeseburger	335
Deluxe	675
Double Cheeseburger	495
Fish Sandwich	468
French Fries, large	381
French Fries, small	239
Hamburger	305
Hot Dog	346
Milkshake	391
Roast Beef Sandwich	390

Jack-in-the-Box

Apple Turnover	411
Breakfast Jack	301
Cheeseburger	
Deluxe	310
Jumbo Jack	628
Double Cheese Omelet	423
French Fries	270
French Toast	537
Hamburger	
Bonus Jack	461
Deluxe	260
Jumbo Jack	551
Ham and Cheese Omelet	425
Jack Burrito	448
Jack Steak	428
Lemon Turnover	446

Moby Jack	455
Onion Rings	351
Pancakes	626
Ranchero Omelet	414
Scrambled Eggs	719
Shakes, Chocolate	365
Strawberry	380
Vanilla	342
Taco	189
Taco Super	285

Kentucky Fried Chicken

Chicken Dinner
   (3 pieces chicken, potatoes, cole slaw, roll)

Original Recipe Dinner	830
Extra Crispy Dinner	950

Individual Pieces

Wing	151
Drumstick	136
Keel	253
Rib	242
Thigh	276

Long John Silver's

Breaded Clams	465
Breaded Oysters	460
Chicken planks	458
Cole Slaw	138
Corn on the Cob	174
Fish with Batter, 2 pieces	318
Fries	375

Hush Puppies	153
Ocean Scallops	257
Peg Leg	514
Shrimp	268
Treasure Chest	467

McDonald's

Apple Pie	300
Big Mac	541
Cheeseburger	306
Cherry Pie	298
Chocolate Shake	364
Egg McMuffin	352
English Muffin, Buttered	186
Fillet O' Fish	402
French Fries	211
Hamburger	257
Hot Cakes, with Butter or Syrup	472
McDonaldland Cookies	294
Quarter-pounder	418
Quarter-pounder with Cheese	518
Sausage	184
Scrambled eggs	162
Shake, Strawberry	345
Shake, Vanilla	323

***Pizza Hut*, 1 slice, Thin**

Standard

Cheese	180
Pepperoni	202
Pork and Mushroom	196

Shrimp Salad	640
Tuna Salad	640

Steak 'N Shake

Steakburger	276
Steakburger with Cheese	352
Super Steakburger	375
Super Steakburger with Cheese	451
Triple Steakburger	474
Triple Steakburger with Cheese	625
Low Calorie Platter	293
Baked Ham Sandwich	451
Toasted Cheese Sandwich	250
Ham & Egg Sandwich	434
Egg Sandwich	275
French Fries	211
Chili and Oyster Crackers	337
Chili	402
Baked Beans	173
Lettuce and Tomato Salad with 1 oz Thousand Island Dressing	168
Chef Salad	313
Cottage Cheese	93
Apple Danish	391
Sundaes	
Strawberry	329
Hot Fudge Nut	530
Brownie Fudge	645
Apple Pie	407
Cherry Pie	334

Cheesecake	368
Brownie	259

Taco Bell

Bean Burrito	343
Beef Burrito	466
Beefy Tostada	291
Bellbeefer	221
Bellbeefer with Cheese	278
Burrito Supreme	457
Combination Burrito	404
Enchirito	454
Pintos Cheese	168
Taco	186
Tostada	179

Wendy's

Cheeseburger	
Single cheese	580
Double cheese	800
Triple cheese	1,040
Chili	230
French Fries	330
Frosty	390
Hamburger	
Single	470
Double	670
Triple	850

White Castle

Cheeseburger	185
Fish	192

French Fries	225
Hamburger	160

Zantiago

Burrito	345
Enchirito	391
Frijoles	231
Taco	146
Tostada	206

CHAPTER 14

Home Cooked, Restaurant and Frozen

HOME COOKED AND RESTAURANT DISHES,
1 average portion unless noted

Ambrosia	126
Ambrosia salad	542
Anchovy butter, 1 Tbsp	127
Angel Food Cake	120
Apples, baked	225
Apples, stuffed	265
Apple Brown Betty	547
Apples, candied	355
Apple Caramel	488
Apple cinnamon rings	180
Apple curried rings	155
Apple fried rings	165
Apple, pickled, 1 apple	50
Applesauce	225
Apple turnovers	400
Apricot, Brown Betty	498
Armenian style mussels, stuffed with rice, currants and piñon nuts	528
Arroz con Pollo	655
Artichoke, boiled	146
Artichoke hearts, marinated	75
Artichokes, Jerusalem boiled	163
Artichoke moutarde	374
Artichoke, Provencal-style, braised	127
Artichoke vinaigrette	446
Asparagus, buttered	90
Asparagus, Chinese-style	150
Asparagus Divan, 4 spears	375
Asparagus vinaigrette	170

Aspic	25
tomato	60
Athenian-style braised lamb shoulder	589
Austrian-style cabbage	210
Avgolemono sauce, 1 Tbsp	10
Avocado salad dressing, 1 Tbsp	63
Avocado salad, with Belgian endive	245
with tomato	288
farci, ½	400
de crabe, ½	410
de crevettes, ½	489
mousse	137
vinaigrette, ½	380
Baba Ghanouj, ½ cup	185
Bagel and lox with cream cheese	374
Bahamian style coffee	216
Bahamian style conch chowder	340
Baked Alaska	485
Baklava	350
Banana, baked	200
Banana, flambée	438
Banana tea bread	105
Bannock	119
Barbecued spareribs	500
Barley and mushroom casserole	300
Bavarian Cream	212
Bear, pot roasted	500
Béarnaise sauce, 1 Tbsp	48
Bechamel sauce, 1 Tbsp	36

Beef and Asparagus 929
   and Bean Curd 682
   and Bean Sprouts 646
   and Broccoli 585
   Congee 896
   Consommé, 1 cup 33
   Fondue Bourguignonne 479
   and Green Pepper 444
   Lo Mein 1,042
   and Mushrooms 435
   and Noodles in Brown Bean Sauce 685
   and Oyster Sauce 689
   with Pea Pods and Water Chestnuts 648
   and Mushroom Pirog 720
   Picadillo 400
Beef Brisket 530
Beef Heart, stuffed 475
Beef Kidneys, braised 275
Beef Roasts
   Pot-au-feu 555
   Pot Roast 600
   Pot Roast, French-style 715
   Pot Roast, German-style 650
   Sauerbraten 569
   Yankee Pot Roast 746
Beef Short Ribs 485
Beef Steak
   Bracioulini 423
   Chicken-fried 935
   Chinese-style 345

14

Beets

harvard in sour cream	170
in horseradish	120
pickled, 1 beet	10
Beignet d 'Aubergines, 4 oz	200
Beurre Manié, 1 Tbsp	98
Bhendi Bhaji	85
Bernaise Sauce, 1 Tbsp	46
Billi-Bi	222
Biscuit Tortoni	284
Biscuit, Baking Powder, 1 piece	83
Black Bean dip, 1 Tbsp	36
Black-eyed peas, Southern-style	550
Black forest cake	758
Blancmange	162
Blanquette de Veau	699
Blini, 1 piece	87
with butter	184
with caviar	204
Blintzes, cheese, 1 piece	177
Blood Sausage, 6 oz	708
Blueberry muffins	133
Blueberry waffles	259
Bocconcini	524
Bordelaise sauce, 1 Tbsp	23
Borscht	400
Boston Baked beans	534
Boston Brown Bread, 1 slice	86
Bougatsa, 1 piece	401
Bouillabaisse	600

Bourek, 1 piece	98
Brains with Almonds	653
braised	338
with sherry	570
Brandied Peaches, 1 peach	65
Bratwurst, grilled, 6 oz	500
Bratwurst, sauteed, 6 oz	563
Brandy Alexander pie	680
Brandy sauce, 1 Tbsp	44
hard, 1 Tbsp	115
Brandy snaps, 1 piece	98
Brazilian Black Beans	376
Bread sauce, 1 Tbsp	18
Brioche	201
Broccoli amandine	279
Broccoli with Parmesan	105
Brownie, 1 piece	160
Buche de Noel	684
Buffalo Steak, broiled	400
Bulgar, pilaf	290
plain	277
Buttermilk Biscuits, 1 piece	88
Buttermilk salad dressing, 1 Tbsp	9
Butterscotch Brownie, 1 piece	156
Butterscotch Sauce, 1 Tbsp	71
Burrito with Beans	321
with Chili	251
with Beef and Beans	335
Bytky	631

Cabbage

Austrian	227
Baked	106
Colcannon	144
Creole	133
Flemish Red, with Apples	268
Pennsylvania Dutch	155
Pickled, 1 cup	200
Polish	400
Rolls Stuffed with Lamb	372
Sweet and Sour	150
Cacciucco	414
Cacik	100
Caesar salad	299

Cake

Applesauce	205
Cheesecake	424
Cheesecake, Italian style	520
Chocolate	230
Cinnamon and Coffee	135
Coconut cream	240
Devil's food	240
Lemon Chiffon	300
Light Fruit	266
Genoese	120
Marble	195
Petits fours, 1 piece	251
Pineapple Upside-down	255
Rainbow	210
Sachertorte	362

Spice	205
Sponge	100
Wedding	150
Trifle	585
Calamari, Baked	286
Calf's Liver	
sauteed	260
with Bacon	375
with Onions	310
alla Veneziana	310
Cannelloni with Beef	398
with Ricotta	356
with Spinach	397
Cannoli	190
Cantonese fried fish, 4 oz	449
Cantonese Lobster	400
Cantonese Shrimp and Vegetables	372
Capicola, 1 slice	108
Caponata, 1 Tbsp	18
Caramel popcorn ball, 1 piece	212
Carp, Sweet and Sour	332
in Brown Sauce	726
Caviar, 1 oz	89
Carrots with dill, 1 cup	55
Carrot tzimmes	707
Cassoulet	1,000
Catalan beef	776
Cauliflower au gratin	323
Cauliflower salad	180
Caviar au gratin, 2 oz	259

Celeri Rémoulade, 4 oz	303
Celeriac, creamed	213
Ceviche	308
Champ	157
Champignon farci gratinée, 1 piece	135
Chantilly Sauce, 1 Tbsp	75
Chard, pureed	107
Char shu ding	300
Charlotte Russe	458
Chasseur Sauce, 1 Tbsp	31
Cheese Boreks	138
Cheese Dumplings, 1 piece	95
Cheese Fondue	1,000
Cheese straws, 10 pieces	283
Cheese sauce, 1 Tbsp	38
Cheese souffle	327
Cherries Jubilee	200
Chestnuts	
creamed	400
pureed	327
roasted, 6 oz	245
Chicken	
and Almonds	750
and Asparagus	510
Barbecued with Skin and Bones	405
Bhuna	219
and Black Bean Sauce	748
Burmese, in Peanut and Coconut Sauce	845
Cacciatore	468
and Cashews	750

14

Musallam	227
with Mushrooms	528
Pancake, Chinese-style	899
Parmigiana	510
Pizziola	290
Roumanian-style, with Apricots	468
Salad	423
with Snow peas	520
Stew	560
stuffed with rice and mushrooms	362
Sub Gum	638
Sweet and Sour	1,150
Tandoori	366
Teriyaki	878
Tetrazzini	878
Chinese-style, with vegetables	670
Velvet	742
Vino bianco	300
with walnuts	929
Yakitori	253
Zingara	500
and tomato salad	199
Chili	448
Chiles con Queso	327
Chiles Rellenos	442
Chiles de Frijoles	544
Chimichango	288
Chinese style	
Beef	343
Cabbage, quickfried	200

Cabbage, steamed	85
Cabbage, Sweet and Sour	200
Carp, Sweet and Sour	300
Mustard Sauce, 1 Tbsp	5
Egg roll	145
Fried eggs and Rice	324
Fried puffs, 1 piece	86
Fried rice	301
Pork with rice	277
Shrimp with ginger	274
Snow peas	115
Spareribs	565
Sweet and sour sauce, 1 Tbsp	15
Cucumber and soy sauce	62

Chocolate

Chiffon Cake, 1 slice	318
Chip Cookie, 1 piece	75
Eclairs	282
Mousse	316
Profiteroles, 1 piece	153
Sauce, 1 Tbsp	86
Hot Soufflé	339

Chinese fried puffs, 1 piece	86
Chopped Chicken liver, ½ cup	262
Chorizos, 1 link	147

Chutney, 1 Tbsp

Coconut	17
Green Tomato	25
Mango	63

14

Mint	10
Tomato	30
Clams	
Bisque	200
in Black Bean Sauce, Chinese-style, 1	39
Casino, 1 dozen	536
New England Pie	325
Origanata, 1 dozen	440
Red Sauce	301
White Sauce	142
Cockaleekie	95
Cocoa	175
Coconut Macaroon, 1 piece	57
Cod Kedgeree	333
Coleslaw and caraway salad	238
Court Bouillon	4
Couscous, Boiled	305
Beef	567
Chicken	653
Lamb	600
Coquilles Saint-Jacques	475
Cornbread, 1 slice	100
Corn Fritters	249
relish, 1 Tbsp	16
sticks, per stick	100
Corned beef and cabbage	600
Corned beef hash	400
Coulibiac	288
Crab	
Cakes, Maryland-style	257

Cocktail, ½ cup	92
Deviled	398
Legs, Alaska King	297
Louis	767
Meunière, 2	278
Mornay	513
Newburg Imperial	426
Cranberry Nut Bread, 1 slice	136
Cranberry Relish, 1 Tbsp	44
Cranberry sauce, 1 Tbsp	28
Cream Cheese Dip, with Bacon and Horseradish, 1 Tbsp	74
Cream Puff, 1 piece	251
Creme brulee	655
Creme Caramel	280
Crepes, au champignon, 1 piece	178
Crepes, au jambon gratinée, 1 piece	156
Crepes Suzette, 1 piece	208
Crispy Bass, Chinese-style	484
Croissant, 1 piece	90
Croque Madame	710
Croque Monsieur	710
Croquettes de crevette	263
Croquettes de volaille	493
Cucumber and yogurt sauce, 1 Tbsp	5
Crumpet, 1 piece	80
Cumberland sauce, 1 Tbsp	40
Curried	
Beef	415
Beef Triangles, 1 piece	154

Lamb	656
Lamb and dhal	870
Cold lobster	493
Shrimp	504
Custard, baked	162
Custard, floating island	253
Custard, rennet	107
Custard sauce	27
Danish pastry	144
Datenut bread, 1 slice	88
Dhal	229
Deviled Ham, 1 Tbsp	38
Diable sauce, 1 Tbsp	20
Dijonnaise sauce, 1 Tbsp	93
Dips, 1 Tbsp	
Black bean	37
Chili	18
Clam in Cream Cheese	75
Cream cheese, bacon and horseradish	71
Curry	40
Deviled clam	80
Taramasalata	102
Divinity, 1 piece	38
Dolma	225
Doughnut	
chocolate, 1 piece	175
jelly	147
old fashioned	135
Duck	
with Cherry sauce	400

Crispy, Chinese style, 4 oz	820
Eight precious, 4 oz	905
with Orange sauce	490
Peking, 4 oz	835
Pressed, 4 oz	399
Wild roast	256
Szechuan, 4 oz	1,000
Tangerine peel, Chinese-style	782
Dumplings, Chinese-style, 1 piece	95
Dumplings, Peking fried, 1 piece	76
Duxelles sauce, 1 Tbsp	19
East Indian Lentils and Rice	264
Eclairs, 1 piece	285
Eel, jellied	605
Eel and egg pie	623
Eggs	
in Aspic, 1	130
Benedict, 1	286
Custard, steamed Chinese-style	226
Deviled, 1	148
Florentine, 1	165
Foo Yong, 1 foo	322
Fried rice, 1 cup	335
Huevos rancheros, 1	177
Salad	403
Scotch, 1	498
Eggnog, nonalcoholic	243
Eggplant	
Basque-style with peppers and tomatoes	155
Dip, 1 Tbsp	45

Fried	281
Greek-style	195
Greek-style, stuffed	180
Ismir	246
Parmigiana	598
Pisto	135
Ratatouille	510
Stuffed with mushrooms and chickpeas	228
Stuffed with pilaf and raisins	188
Turkish	327
Egg Rolls, Chinese, 1 piece	145
Empanada, with beef	244
Empanada, with chicken	220
Enchilada	
Beef	299
Cheese	270
Chicken	330
Chorizo	267
Escalopes de veau cordon bleu	680
Escargot de bourgogne, 6 pieces	418
Escarole, sautéed	74
Esterhazy steak	994
Falafel	263
Fennel, braised	116
Fettuccine Alfredo	1,550
Fettuccine con Baccala	653
Figs, fresh stewed	195
Finnan Haddie	257
Fish balls, Chinese-style, 8 oz	319

Fish, Jade Chinese-style, 6 oz	547
Lemon Chinese-style, 8 oz	754
Fish mousse	286
Fish piquant en papillote	199
Fish soufflé	300
Flan	263
Flemish red cabbage and apples	248
Floating island	257
Florentines, 1 piece	118
Flounder fillet in black bean sauce	600
Fondue de Gruyère	478
Fragrant noodles with shrimp, Chinese-style	810
Franks in blankets, 1 piece	46
French-fried onion rings	165
French-fried potatoes	227
Frijoles fritos	325
Frijoles Mexicanos	194
Frikadeller	384
Fruit cake, light, 1 slice	264
Fudge, chocolate, 1 piece	78
Fudge Sauce, hot, 1 Tbsp	100
Garlic bread, 1 slice	88
Garlic sauce, 1 Tbsp	11
Gefilte fish	183
Giblet gravy, 1 Tbsp	16
Gingersnaps, 1 piece	97
Gingerbread, 1 slice	206
Gingerbread boys, 1 boy	132
Gnocchi, Cheese	410

Farina parmigiana	385
Potato	314
Goose, Braised with chestnuts and onions	525
German style stuffed with potatoes	488
Roasted with apples and sauerkraut stuffing	842
Goulash	394
Grand Marnier soufflé	262
Grand Marnier with strawberries	110
Granite, 1 cup	263
Grasshopper pie	680
Gravy, 1 Tbsp	
au jus	4
giblet	15
mushroom	22
Greek Salad	235
Greek Gyro	246
Green Olives, 2 large	20
Green Beans with garlic, Chinese-style	205
Green Goddess dressing, 1 Tbsp	89
Grenouilles a l'Anglaise	385
Meuniere	485
Provencale	423
Green pepper, Stuffed	190
with beef and kidney beans	356
Mexican-style	444
Green sauce, 1 Tbsp	82
Grits	150
Guacamole, 1 Tbsp	28
Gumbo, corn	172

Gumbo, shrimp	308
Haddock, Baked	300
Creamy smoked and potato casserole	425
Ham	
in aspic	600
fried with red eye gravy	400
loaf	427
Tetrazzini	590
Hamburger	
bacon	400
broiled	280
cheese	370
chili	285
Pizza	285
mushroom	270
Hash	310
Hawaiian spareribs	409
Herb Butter, 1 Tbsp	125
Herring	
and beets a la Russe	591
in dill sauce	188
in mustard sauce	150
in oatmeal	370
Pickled	217
Rollmops	239
Scandanavian salad	379
in sour cream	127
Hoagie, 1 roll	400
Hog Jowl and Black-Eyed Peas	351
Hollandaise sauce, 1 Tbsp	48

Horseradish cream sauce, 1 Tbsp	77
Horseradish, fresh, 1 Tbsp	5
Hot Chocolate	275
Hot Cross Bun, 1 piece	105
Huevos Rancheros, 1 egg	186
Humus with tahini, ½ cup	364
Hushpuppies, 1 piece	67
Indian Corn Fritters, 1 piece	50
Indian Pudding	371
Indian Rice Pilaf	395
Irish Soda Bread, 1 slice	114
Irish Stew	710
Japanese Salad	
autumn	150
cucumber	48
cucumber and fish	135
cucumber and seaweed	64
lotus root	87
Jelly, homemade, 1 Tbsp	45
Jelly Roll	187
Jhinga Bhajia, 1 piece	37
Jhinga Kari, 10-12 shrimp	609
Jhonnycake, 1 piece	98
Kasha, buckwheat	355
appel-almond	400
Katsudon	829
Kebabs, Indian lamb	231
Kedgeree	318
Keema curry	246
Keftedakia Marinata	410

Keftedes	248
Keftedes Avgolemono	200
Khiri Pachadi	122
Kibbeh	964
Kidneys, braised	289
Kielbasa, fried, 3 oz	350
Kissel	240
Knockwurst, sauteed, 6 oz	538
Korma curry	344
Koulebiaka	1,300
Kourabiedes, 1 piece	75
Kreplach, 1 piece	34
Kugelhupf, 1 slice	187
Ladyfingers, 1 piece	52
Lamb	
braised	490
breast	425
cassoulet	1,050
crown roast	270
dolma	232
kidneys in sour cream	485
riblets, barbecued	840
shanks	372
shish kebab	686
stew	403
Lancashire Hot Pot	552
Lasagne, with cheese	605
with meat	408
with meat balls	1,095
Lebkuchen, 1 piece	84

Moo goo gai pan	244
Mornay sauce, 1 Tbsp	33
Moules	
farcis provencale, 8–10 pieces	324
gratinées Normande, 8–10 pieces	285
Marseille, 8–10 pieces	450
salade de, 8–10 pieces	461
vinaigrette, 8–10 pieces	230
Moussaka	818
Mousse, Avocado	196
Chocolate	306
Fish	282
Mozzarella cheese, breaded and fried	231
Muffin, 1 piece	108
Bran	140
Corn	148
Raisin bran	162
Mushroom gravy, 1 Tbsp	26
Mushrooms	
creamed	200
in madeira	236
marinated	51
sauteed	187
Mushrooms with bamboo shoots	295
Mu shu pork, 2 pancakes	874
Mustard sauce, 1 Tbsp	41
Nachos, 1 piece	40
Nantua sauce, 1 Tbsp	24
Napoleons, 1 piece	402

Napolitos	100
New England boiled dinner	735
Nockerln	163
Noodles in brown bean sauce and pork	891
Noodles in oyster sauce	463
Normandy rock cornish game hen, 1 bird	700
Oatmeal Bread, 1 slice	120
Octopus Mediterranean	350
Okra, fried	175
Omelet	
with caviar, 1 egg	180
Greek, 1 egg	130
Lorraine, 1 egg	167
Lyonnaise, 1 egg	136
with mushroom and tomato, 1 egg	135
Onion frittata, 1 egg	200
Piperade, 1 egg	215
Soufflé, 1 egg	111
Spanish, 1 egg	127
Onion Rings, french-fried	184
Onions, baked, 1 piece	155
Onions, creamed	209
sautéed	150
stuffed	186
Oshi tashi	34
Osso buco	905
Oysters casino, 1 dozen	540
Oysters en Brochette	215
Oysters Rockefeller, 1 dozen	1,000

14

Oyster Sauce, 1 Tbsp	35
Paella	
with lobster	620
with sausage	630
Valenciana	548
Pakora (Indian fritters)	
Baigon	41
Gobhi	38
Mixed vegetable	54
Pancakes, 1 piece	
apple	95
blueberry	87
buckwheat	82
buttermilk	73
pecan	135
plain	85
wholewheat	89
Panettone, 1 slice	322
Paper-wrapped Chicken, Chinese-style, 1 piece	98
Parsley sauce, 1 Tbsp	22
Parsnips, roasted	211
Pashka	300
Pastitsio	820
Pâté	
de Campagne	584
de Canard	1,076
de Foie Gras	648
de Poisson au Asperges	478
Peach	
cardinal	230

cobbler	500
Melba	354
Peanut brittle, 1 piece	77
Peanut butter cookies, 1 piece	70
Pea pods with water chestnuts	307
Pea pods with mushrooms	261
Pear Helene	602
Peking custard	464
Penuche, 1 piece	41
Pepper, Greek stuffed green	120
Pepper, Greek stuffed with rice	160
Peppermint sauce, 1 Tbsp	46
Pepperoni, 1 slice	26
Pfeffernusse, 1 piece	82
Picadillo	400
Piccalilli, 1 Tbsp	12
Pie	
Apple, country	410
Apple, deep dish	445
Banana Cream	626
Blueberry	475
Boston Cream	265
Chocolate cream	610
Coconut cream	462
Coconut custard	400
Key Lime	693
Lemon Meringue	545
Nesselrode	516
Peach	400
Pecan	585

Pumpkin	400
Shoofly	528
Pigeon Pie	587
Pig's feet, 1 foot	251
Pigs in blanket	200
Pilaf	
Bulgur	306
Lamb	572
Rice	312
Piquante sauce, 1 Tbsp	19
Pirog, Beef and Mushroom	727
Piroshki	155
Pissaladiere	474
Pita bread	247
Pizza, 1 slice	
Plain	450
Green peppers	452
Mushrooms	462
Pepperoni	587
Plantains	136
Plum pudding, Steamed	451
Plum sauce, 1 Tbsp	30
Polenta	88
Pollo en Salsa verde	244
Pollo molé verde	367
Popcorn balls, 1 ball	249
Poppy seed bread sticks, 1 piece	18
Pork	
Balls, steamed, Chinese-style	488
Barbecued	357

Barbecued with vegetables, Chinese-style	640
Breaded, Italian-style	423
Choucroute garnie	1,000
with rice, Spanish-style	481
Crown roast	584
Loin, stuffed with apples and prunes	685
Lo mein	849
Red, cooked with chestnuts, Chinese-style	432
Sliced, Chinese-style	306
Sliced with green pepper, Chinese-style	411
Soong	666
Spareribs, barbecued	415
Spareribs, Chinese	555
Stuffed with oysters	400
Subgum chow mein	322
Suckling pig	1,100
Sweet and sour, Chinese-style	643
Sweet and sour stew	629
Szechuan-style with bean curd	576
Tenderloin, roast	345
Twice cooked in brown sauce	625
Twice cooked in Hoisin sauce	548
Teriyaki	453
Portugese Filhos, 1 piece	45
Potato Bread, 1 slice	70
Potatoes	
Anna	186
Au Gratin	310
Dauphine	268
Duchess	209

Saltimbocca	520
Sandwiches	
Bacon, lettuce, and tomato	268
Bagel with cream cheese	255
Bagel with lox and cream cheese	355
Bologna	355
Cheese, grilled	400
Cheese, grilled with bacon	543
Cheese, grilled with tomato	415
Chopped liver	382
Corned beef	446
Fried egg	225
Lobster salad	255
Meatball with tomato sauce	400
Meatloaf	300
Monte Cristo	920
Pastrami	560
Roast beef, overstuffed	490
Reuben	582
Salami	394
Shrimp salad	250
Steak	353
Tongue, overstuffed	475
Tuna fish salad	324
Turkey club	505
Sangria	93
Sardine Fraiches Marines, 4 oz	328
Sashimi, assorted, 4 oz	100
tako, 4 oz	87
Sate	500

Sauce Supreme, 1 Tbsp	34
Saucisson rémoulade	631
Sauerbraten	570
Sauerkraut, with juniper berries, braised	257
with caraway seeds	72
Sausage and Peppers, 2 pieces	882
Scallops, broiled	210
en Brochette	254
Scampi	178
Scrapple	288
Scungilli marinara	269
Sfogliatelli	244
Shabu-shabu	448
Shepherd's Pie	500
Shish kebab	679
Shortbread, Scottish	152
Shortcake, strawberry	591
Shrimp	
Ajillo, 8 large	466
in almond sauce, 8 large	333
Balls, Chinese-style	286
Batter-fried, Chinese-style, 1 piece	84
with bean curd, 12 medium	980
with black bean sauce, Chinese-style	464
Braised, Chinese-style 12 medium	905
Butterfly, Japanese-style	250
with cashews	536
creole	344
Egg foo yong	356
Fried in shell, Chinese-style, 12 medium	674

Glass	299
in green sauce, Spanish-style 8–10	290
Gumbo	327
Jumbalaya	500
in lobster sauce, Chinese-style, 12 medium	1,250
lo mein	501
with Mexican Chilis, 8–10	401
Newburg	600
One shrimp two flavors, 14 medium	900
Scampi	180
Stir-fried, 12 medium	738
Shu Mai, 1 piece	45
Sweet and sour, 12 medium	1,900
Szechuan pepper	324
Toast, 1 piece	162
Sloppy Joe	318
Snails a la bourguignonne, 1 dozen	320
Snails a la provencale, 1 dozen	300
Sole À L'Américaine	305
Amandine	509
Bonne femme	550
with Crab Sauce	300
Goujons de	460
Meuniere	490
Veronique	600
Sopapilla	128
Sopapilla with honey and cream	209
Soubise sauce, 1 Tbsp	20
Soufflé	
au fromage	197

Clam chowder, New England	283
Chicken noodle	78
Chicken and rice	78
Chicken with bean curd, Japanese-style	74
Consommé	42
Escarole	138
Garlic	197
Gazpacho	192
Hungarian cherry	375
Hungarian cream of barley	204
Minestrone	243
Miso with bean curd	79
Miso with fish balls	142
Mulligatawny	304
Mushroom, cream of	272
Oxtail	329
Pastina	134
Peanut, cream of	520
Potato	209
Pumpkin	150
Sauerkraut	128
Senegalese	314
Stracciatelli	125
Stschy	167
Tortellini	210
Turtle, home style	278
Vegetable, cream of	340
Sour cream and chive, 1 Tbsp	29
Sour Dough Bread, 1 slice	65
Souvlaki	291

Spaghetti, 1 cup

Alfredo	405
Bolognese	357
with butter, cream and parmesan	401
Carbonara	860
Clam sauce, red	300
Clam sauce, white	344
Fagioli	348
with meatballs in sauce	853
Paglia e fieno	506
al pesto	980
Pomodoro	268
with sausage	471
Spatzle	165
Spiedini with anchovy	386
Spinach au gratin	275
Spinach, creamed	144
Spoon bread	632
Spumoni, 1 cup	510
Squid, Mediterranean	390
Stuffed with Rice, Greek-style	354
Squirrel Stew	500
Steamed Chinese sausage	778
Steamed Scallops with cabbage, Chinese-style, 8 pieces	300
Steamed Whole Fish, Chinese-style, 1 lb	902
Stifado	228
Stollen, 1 slice	145
Strawberries Romanoff	322
Strawberry Shortcake	500

Strudel
Almond	398
Apple	360
Cheese	410
Cherry	405
Poppy seed	400

Stuffing, 1 cup
Chestnut and mushroom	472
Corn bread	700
Herbed	210
Rice	263
Sage and onion	220

Submarine, 1 roll	381
Sukiyaki	348

Sushi
Chirashi	460
Norimaki	468
Tekka maki	400

Sweet and Sour Chinese meatballs	936
Sweet and Sour fish, 1 lb	902
Sweet and Sour sauce, 1 Tbsp	20
Tabbouleh	304

Tacos
Bean	275
Cheese	205
Chicken	245
Chili	348
Chorizo	367

Taffy, 1 piece	50
Tahini sauce, ¼ cup	167

Tamale pie	268
Tandoori fish	300
Shrimp, 10–12	288
Taramasalata, 1 Tbsp	100
Tartar sauce, 1 Tbsp	92
Tarte au champignon	382
au Oignons	570
Tea Eggs, 1 egg	85
Tempura	590
Tempura sauce, 1 Tbsp	5
Teriyaki	
Beef	213
Chicken	380
Pork	462
Teriyaki sauce, 1 Tbsp	15
Toad in the Hole	700
Toast, French, 1 slice	143
Toll House Cookies, 1 piece	60
Tomato Aspic	73
Tomatos, broiled	126
Tomato sauce, 1 Tbsp	10
Bolognese, 1 cup	330
Italian-style, 1 cup	215
with red clam, 1 cup	300
Tomatos, stewed	43
Tortellini with butter and parmesan	582
with ricotta and cream	600
Tortillas, 1 piece, plain	75
Chili	196
Chorizo	500

Sweetbreads

braised	300
creamed	535
with mushrooms	575
sauteed	200
with sherry	585
Terrine of Veal and Ham	250
Vitello Tonnata	850
a la zingara	602
Venison Burgers	360
Ragout of	437
Roast saddle of	205
Vichyssoise	410
Vinaigrette, 1 Tbsp	100
Weiner Schnitzel	415
a la Holstein	457
White sauce, 1 cup	400
Wild Boar, pot roast	500
Wild Duck, roasted	265
Won ton, fried sweet, 1 piece	59
Yakinasu, 4 oz	38
Yakitori	263
Yakitori donburi	781
Yam, candied	315
Yankee pot roast	775
Yogurt kholodnyk	40
Yogurt sauce, 1 Tbsp	9
Yorkshire Pudding	78
Yorkshire Scones, 1 piece	150
Yudofu	83

Zabaglione	177
Zeppole, 1 piece	42
Zucchini, Fried, 1 strip	37
Italian style	100
Sautéed, ½ cup	71
Zuppa di pesce	458
Zuppa Inglese	378

FROZEN DINNERS,

1 complete dinner (see also pp 141-144 and pp 150-153)

Beans and Franks	
Banquet	591
Morton	530
Swanson	550
Beef	
Banquet	312
Chopped	443
La Choy	342
Lean Cuisine Oriental	280
Morton	270
Chopped	340

Country Table	540
Steak House	920
Swanson	370
3-Course	490
Chopped	460
Hungry Man	540
Hungry Man 18 oz	730
Weight Watchers 10 oz	387
Weight Watchers 16 oz	586
Beef and Beans	
Swanson	500
Beef Stroganoff	
Stouffer's	390
Chicken	
La Choy	354
Morton	240
Swanson boneless	730
Weight Watchers	330
Chicken and Biscuits	
Green Giant	200
Chicken Croquettes	
Morton	410
Chicken Cacciatore	
Stouffer's	313
Weight Watchers	356
Chicken and Dumplings	
Banquet	282
Morton	280
Chicken, fried	
Banquet	530

Man Pleaser	1,026
Morton	470
Country Table	710
Swanson	570
3-Course	630
Hungry Man	620
Hungry Man, 15¼ oz	910
Hungry Man, Barbecue	760
Crispy Fried	650
Chicken, glazed	
Lean Cuisine	270
Chicken with noodles	
Morton	260
Chicken, oriental	
Weight Watchers	320
Chicken Parmigiana and Spinach	
Weight Watchers	200
Chicken and vegetables	
Lean Cuisine	260
Chop Suey	
Banquet	282
Chow Mein	
Banquet	282
Green Giant	130
Lean Cuisine	240
Enchilada	
Banquet	
Beef	479
Cheese	459
El Chico	680

Swanson	570
Van de Kamp	
Beef	420
Cheese	430
Fish	
Banquet	382
Haddock	419
Perch	434
Lean Cuisine	200
Morton	270
Weight Watchers	
Flounder	240
Haddock	250
Perch	320
Sole	240
Turbot	490
Fish and Chips	
Swanson	450
Hungry Man	760
Ham	
Banquet	369
Morton	440
Swanson	380
Hash	
Banquet	372
Italian	
Banquet	446
Swanson	420
Lasagna	
Lean Cuisine Zucchini Lasagne	260

Lean Line	270
Swanson	740
Macaroni and beef	
Banquet	394
Morton	260
Swanson	400
Macaroni and cheese	
Banquet	326
Morton	320
Swanson	390
Manicotti	
Lean Line	270
Meat Loaf	
Banquet	412
Morton	340
Country Table	480
Swanson	530
Meatball	
Swanson	400
Mexican	
Banquet	571
Combination	571
El Chico	820
Swanson	600
Pepper	
La Choy	349
Polynesian	
Swanson	490
Pork	
Swanson	470

Queso
El Chico   810
Salisbury Steak
Banquet   390
Morton   290
Country Table   430
Swanson   - 790
3-Course   490
Hungry Man   870
Saltillo
El Chico   790
Sausage with veal, 1 link
Lean Line   90
Stuffed Shells
Lean Line   260
Shrimp
La Choy   325
Spaghetti with beef
Lean Cuisine   280
Spaghetti and meatball
Banquet   450
Morton   360
Swanson   410
Hungry Man   660
Swiss Steak
Swanson   350
Tacos, beef
El Chico   410
Turkey
Banquet   293

Man Pleaser	620
Morton	350
Country Table	600
Swanson	360
3-Course	520
Hungry Man	740
Weight Watchers	400
Veal Parmigiana	
Banquet	421
Morton	330
Swanson	520
Hungry Man	910
Weight Watchers	230
Western	
Banquet	417
Morton	410
Swanson	460
Hungry Man	890
Ziti, baked	
Lean Line	270

CHAPTER 15

Fingertip Low Calorie Guide

. OVER 350 CALORIES

Frozen entrees (at less than 30 calories per ounce)

Banquet Buffet Supper Beef and Noodles, 32 oz	754
Banquet Buffet Supper Beef Stew, 32 oz	700
Banquet Buffet Supper Chicken and Noodles, 32 oz	764
Banquet Buffet Supper Beef sliced with gravy, 32 oz	782
Banquet Buffet Supper Turkey, 32 oz	564
La Choy Chicken	354

Morton Country Table Salisbury Steak, 15 oz	430
Swanson Hungry-Man Turkey, 13¼ oz	380
Weight Watchers Turkey Tetrazzini, 13 oz	380

200-350 CALORIES

Frozen entrees (at less than 30 calories per ounce)

Beef

Banquet, 11 oz	312
Lean Cuisine, 9⅛ oz	280
Morton, 10 oz	270

Chicken

Morton, 10 oz	240
Stouffer's	
Chicken a la King, 9½ oz	330
Creamed Chicken, 6½ oz	300
Chicken Divan, 8½ oz	335
Weight Watchers, 15 oz	330

Chicken and Biscuits

Green Giant, 7 oz	200

Chicken Creole

Weight Watchers, 13 oz	250

Chicken and Dumplings

Banquet, 12 oz	282
Morton, 11 oz	280

Chicken with Noodles
Green Giant, 9 oz   250
Morton, 10½ oz   260

Chicken Oriental
Weight Watchers, 16 oz   320

Chicken Parmigiana and Spinach
Weight Watchers, 9 oz   200

Chicken and Vegetables
Lean Cuisine, 12¾ oz   260

Chicken White Meat with Peas
Weight Watchers, 9 oz   270

Chop Suey
Banquet, 12 oz   282

Chow Mein
Banquet, 12 oz   282
Lean Cuisine, 11¼ oz   240

Eggplant Parmigiana
Weight Watchers, 13 oz   280

Fish
Lean Cuisine, 9 oz   200
Morton, 9 oz   270
Weight Watchers
    Flounder, 16 oz   240
    Haddock, 16 oz   250
    Perch, 16 oz   320
    Sole, 16 oz   240
    Sole with peas, mushrooms and
      lobster sauce, 9½ oz   200

Green Peppers with Beef
Green Giant, 7 oz   200

Lasagne
Lean Line, 10 oz   270
Lasagne, Zucchini
Lean Cuisine, 11 oz   260
Macaroni with Beef
Green Giant, 9 oz   240
Morton, 10 oz   260
Macaroni and Cheese
Banquet, 12 oz   326
Morton, 11 oz   320
Manicotti
Lean Line, 11 oz   270
Salisbury Steak
Banquet, 11 oz   390
Morton, 11 oz   290
Shells, Stuffed
Lean Line, 11 oz   260
Spaghetti with Beef
Lean Cuisine, 11½ oz   280
Turkey
Banquet, 11 oz   293
Swanson Turkey Slices, 8¾ oz   260
Ziti, Baked
Lean Line, 10 oz   270
Ziti with Veal and sauce
Weight Watchers, 13 oz   350
Veal Parmigiana with Zucchini
Weight Watchers, 9½ oz   230

Canned Entrees (at less than 30 calories per ounce)

Pasta, one can
  Ravioli
    Franco-American Beef, 7½ oz   220
  Rotini
    Franco-American, 7½ oz   200
  Macaroni
    Franco-American, 7½ oz   220
  Macaroni and Meatballs
    Franco-American, 7½ oz   220
Meat, one can
  Beef Goulash
    Hormel, 7½ oz   240
  Ham, whole
    Hormel, 6 oz   312
  Tuna, in water, drained
    Chicken of the Sea solid white, 7 oz can   216

Fish, Fresh

Crab, steamed, meat only, 8 oz   211
Haddock, fillets, 8 oz   180
Halibut, fillets, 8 oz   226
Oysters, Pacific and Western, meat only, 8 oz   207

15
Meat

Beef
Chuck
  boneless, lean only, braised, 4 oz   219
  boneless, lean only, stewed, 4 oz   243
Flank steak, boneless, all lean, braised, 4 oz   222
ground, lean with 10% fat, 4 oz   203
porterhouse steak with 9% bone, lean only,
  broiled, 4 oz without bone   254
round steak, boneless, lean only, braised or
  broiled, 4 oz   296
sirloin steak, 7% bone, lean only, broiled,
  4 oz without bone   235
T-bone, 11% bone, lean only, broiled, 4 oz
  without bone   253

Ham
fresh, lean only
  baked, without bone and skin, 4 oz   246
light cured, lean only
  baked, without bone and skin, 4 oz   328

Lamb
Leg, lean only, roasted, boneless, 4 oz   211
loin chops, with bone, lean only, broiled,
  4 oz   213
rib chops, with bone, lean only, broiled,
  4 oz   239
shoulder, lean only, roasted, boneless, 4 oz   233

Pork

Picnic, without bone and skin, lean only, baked
or roasted, 4 oz   239

Veal

loin cuts, lean with fat, braised or broiled,
without bone, 4 oz   245

round with rump (roasts and leg cutlets),
lean with fat, braised or broiled, without
bone, 4 oz   245

Poultry

Chicken

roasted, without skin, 4 oz   204
stewed, light meat without skin, 4 oz   207
Turkey, roasted, light meat without skin, 4 oz   200

101-200 CALORIES

Pasta

All pasta, dry, one cup
cooked till tender, (approx)   190
cooked till firm, (approx)   155

Canned, 1 can

Franco-American macaroni and cheese, 7½ oz   184

Franco-American spaghetti with cheese, 7⅜ oz   170

Franco-American spaghetti with cheese
sauce, 7⅜ oz   160

Meat Entrees (at less than 30 calories per ounce)

Frozen

Beef, chipped, creamed

Banquet, 5 oz   124

Beef, sliced

Banquet, barbecue sauce, 5 oz   126

Banquet, with gravy, 5 oz   116

Green Giant, 5 oz   130

Beef Stew

Green Giant Boil-in-Bag, 9 oz   160

Green Giant, with biscuits, 7 oz   190

Veal steaks

Hormel, 4 oz   130

Meat Entrees, canned (at less than 30 calories per ounce), 1 can

Beef, corned with cabbage
   Hormel, 8 oz   150
Beef stew
   Dinty Moore, 7½ oz   184
   Swanson, 7½ oz   190
Pork, sliced, with gravy
   Morton House, 6¼ oz   190

Poultry entrees

Frozen (at less than 30 calories per ounce)
   Chicken a la King
      Banquet, 5 oz   138
Canned, 1 can
   Chicken stew
      Swanson, 7½ oz   180
   Turkey slices
      Morton House, 6¼ oz   140
   Chicken, fresh
      Broiled, meat only, 4 oz   154

15 Seafood

Clams, canned, drained, 1 can
   Doxsee, 8 oz   112
   Doxsee, 12 oz   147
Shrimp marinara, with shells, frozen
   Buitoni, 4 oz   116

Fish, fresh, 4 oz, meat only

Abalone	111
Black Sea Bass	106
Butterfish, gulf	108
Catfish, fresh water	117
Croaker, Atlantic	109
Lake Herring (Cisco)	109
Lobster	109
Mussels	108
Ocean Pearch, Pacific	108
Red or Grey Snapper	106
Sea bass, white	109
Shrimp	103
Sturgeon	107
Tautog (Blackfish)	101

51-100 CALORIES

Miscellaneous

Pabst Extra Light Beer	70
Whipped butter, 1 Tbsp	65
Farina, *Pillsbury*, ⅔ cup	80
Grits, *Quaker* Instant, 1 packet	79
One Egg, raw or boiled	
extra large	94
large	82
medium	72
Canned Spaghetti with meatballs, *Libby's*, 1 cup	84
Canned Spanish rice, *Libby's*, 1 cup	57

Chinese dishes

Chow mein, canned, 1 cup	
La Choy	
beef	72
chicken	68
mushroom	85
pepper	89
shrimp	61
Chow mein, frozen	
Banquet, 1 bag	89

La Choy beef, 1 cup	97
La Choy shrimp, 1 cup	73
Pea pods, frozen, 1 package	
La Choy	90
Won Ton, frozen, 1 cup	
La Choy	92

Dairy

Cottage Cheese, low fat, ½ cup	
Borden	90
Breakstone	90
Friendship	100
Lucerne	100
Viva	100
Weight Watchers	90
Milk, 8 ounces	
Buttermilk	
.1% fat *Borden*	88
.2% fat *Sealtest* skim	71
.5% fat *Borden*	90
.8% fat *Golden Nugget*	92
.8% fat *Light 'n Lively*	95
Dry, non-fat milk, reconstituted	81
Skin or low-fat	
no fat *Lucerne*	90
.1% fat *Borden*	81

fortified	81
.1% fat *Sealtest*	79
Yogurt, plain, ½ cup	
Borden Lite-Line lowfat	70
Sealtest Light 'n Lively lowfat	70
Danny On-A-Stick, uncoated	65

Meat, canned

Beef stew	
Libby's, 1 cup	78
Ham, whole	
Wilson's certified boned and rolled, 1 oz	56

Poultry

Chicken stew with dumplings, canned	
Libby's, 1 cup	88
Turkey with gravy, frozen	
Banquet, 5 oz	98
Green Giant, 5 oz	100

Seafood, canned

Clams
Snow's, ½ cup	60
Sau-Sea, 4 oz	99

Gefilte Fish
Manischewitz, 3 oz piece	53
Manischewitz whitefish and pike, 3 oz piece	64
Mother's, 4 oz piece	55

Oysters
Bumblebee, ½ cup	86

Shrimp
Bumblebee, 4½ oz can	90

Seafood, fresh, meat only, 4 oz

Clams	92
Cod	88
Crayfish	82
Croaker, white	95
Flounder	89
Ocean Perch, Atlantic	100
Oysters	75
Pickerel	95
Pike	100
Sand Dab	89
Sauger	95
Scallops	92
Sole	90
Squid	95
Tilefish	90

Fruits and Vegetables

Artichokes
  boiled, drained, 1 whole bud   67
Beets
  raw, diced, 1 cup   58
Broccoli
  boiled, drained, 8 oz   59
Carrots
  raw, slices, 1 cup   53
Chayote
  raw, 1 medium squash   56
Cranberries
  fresh, without stems, 1 cup   52
Currants, red or white
  trimmed, 1 cup   55
Dock or Sorrel
  raw with stems, 1 lb   89
Endive, French or Belgian
  trimmed, 1 lb   68
Escarole
  untrimmed, 1 lb   80
Grapefruit
  pink or red, with seeds
    whole, with skin, 1 lb   87
    sections, 1 cup   80
  pink or red, seedless
    whole, with skin, 1 lb   93
    sections, 1 cup   80

white, with seeds
  whole, with skin, 1 lb   84
  sections, 1 cup   82
white, seedless
  whole, with skin, 1 lb   87
  sections, 1 cup   78

Honeydew Melon
whole, with rinds and seeds, 1 lb   94
cubed or diced, 1 cup   56

Lettuce
Iceberg
  whole, 1 lb   56
Loose Leaf
  whole, 1 lb   52
Romaine or cos
  whole, 1 lb   52

Pawpaw
peeled and seeded, 4 oz   96

Papaya
peeled and seeded, cubed, 1 cup   55

Peaches
pared, sliced, 1 cup   65

Raspberries
black, 1 cup   98
red, 1 cup   70

Strawberries
whole, 1 cup   55

Watermelon
whole, with rind, 1 lb   54

20-50 CALORIES

Breads, Buns and Rolls

Bread, 1 slice
Gluten
Thomas 32
Protein
Thomas 45
Rice Cakes
Spiral 36
Wheat
Thomas 50
White
Arnold Melba Thin 40
Fresh Horizons 50
Pepperidge Farm Very Thin 40
Weight Watchers 35
Buns and Rolls, 1 piece
Pepperidge Farm Old-Fashioned 37
Pepperidge Farm Party 35
Margarine, 1 Tbsp
Blue Bonnet Diet 50
Fleischmann Diet 50
Imitation 50

15

Candy, 1 piece

Rolo   28

Cheese, 1 oz

Farmer's
Friendship   38
Ricotta
Borden   42
Imitation Cream Cheese
Philadelphia   50
American, grated
Borden   30

Chinese Dishes

Apple-Cinnamon roll, frozen
La Choy, 1 piece   38
Bamboo Shoots, canned
La Choy, 8 oz   23
Bean sprouts, canned
La Choy, 8 oz   24
Chow Mein, canned, 1 cup
Chun King   44
La Choy, meatless   47

Egg Rolls, frozen
La Choy chicken, 1 piece	30
La Choy lobster, 1 piece	27

Mixed vegetables, canned
La Choy, 1 cup	35

Cream

Half & Half, 1 Tbsp
	20
Lucerne Real Cream topping, 1 whipped oz	20

Dips, 1 oz

Bean, Jalapeño
Frito-Lay	36
Gebhardt	30
Granny Goose	37
Lucerne	36

Clam
Lucerne	34

Gelatin
Knox gelatin, 1 envelope	28

Gravy
French's Pork, mix, ½ cup	40

15

Jelly, 1 Tbsp

Apple
  Kraft, Low Calorie   22
  Diet Delight   22
Apricot Pineapple Jam
  Diet Delight   21
Blackberry Apple
  Kraft, low calorie   22
Blackberry Jam
  Diet Delight   21
Grape
  Kraft, Low Calorie   22
  Diet Delight   21
Raspberry Jam
  Diet Delight   21

Meat, 1 oz, canned

Beef
  Corned, canned
    Safeway   35
  Dried
    Swift   42
  Smoked
    Safeway   35
    Safeway spicy   40

Beef roast
  Wilson   33
Ham
  Wilson certified fully cooked   48
  Wilson certified *Tender Made*   44
  Wilson certified festival ham   48
Pastrami
  Safeway   40
Scrapple
  Oscar Mayer in tube   50
  Oscar Mayer Philadelphia style   45

Olives

Green, 10 large   45
Manzanillo Black, 10 large   50

Popcorn, 1 cup

Pops-Rite, popped   38
Wise, cheese-flavored, ready to eat   49

15 Poultry

Safeway smoked chicken, 1 oz	50
Safeway smoked turkey, 1 oz	50

Pudding, ½ cup

D-Zerta
butterscotch	25
chocolate	20
vanilla	30

Salad Dressing, 1 Tbsp

French
Ann Page Low Calorie	25
Kraft Low Calorie	25
Nu Made Low Calorie	20

Italian
Wish-Bone Low Calorie	20

May Lo Naise
Tillie Lewis	25

Russian
Wish-Bone Low Calorie	25

Thousand Island
Ann Page. Low Calorie	25
Wish-Bone Low Calorie	25

Whipped
Tillie Lewis	25

Sauces & Spreads

Crosse & Blackwell Anchovy Paste 1 Tbsp	20
***Hunt's* Tomato Sauce, 4 oz**	35
with mushrooms, 4 oz	40
***Open Pit* Barbecue, 1 Tbsp**	26

Vegetables, canned and frozen

Artichoke Hearts
Birds Eye, 3 oz	20

Asparagus, 1 cup, canned
cuts	40
spears	40
spears and tips	35
whole	50

Asparagus, frozen
Birds Eye, 3.3 oz	25
Seabrook Farms, ½ cup	23

15

Beans, green canned, 1 cup
french

Del Monte	40
Green Giant	30
Kounty Kist	40
Libby's	35

whole

Del Monte	35
Green Giant	30
Kounty Kist	40
Libby's	35
Stokely-Van Camp	40

Beans, green, frozen

Birds Eye, 3.3 oz	25
Kounty Kist, 1 cup	30
Seabrook Farms, 1 cup	42

Beans, wax or yellow, 1 cup

Del Monte	35
Libby's	40
Stokely-Van Camp	45

Broccoli, frozen

Birds Eye 3.3 oz	25
Green Giant, 1 cup	30
Kounty Kist, 1 cup	30
Seabrook Farms, 1 cup	46

Brussels Sprouts, frozen

Birds Eye, 3.3 oz	30
Green Giant, 1 cup	50
Kounty Kist, 1 cup	50

Carrots, canned, 1 cup
Libby's   40
S & W   44

Cauliflower, frozen
Birds Eye 3.3 oz   25
Green Giant, 1 cup   25
Kounty Kist, 1 cup   25

Collard Greens
Birds Eye, 3.3 oz   30
Seabrook Farms, 1 cup   44

Mixed Vegetables
Kounty Kist, California, 1 cup   30

Mustard Greens
Seabrook Farms, ½ cup   21

Sauerkraut, canned, 1 cup   50
Spinach, canned, 1 cup   45
Spinach, frozen, 1 cup   50

Tomatoes, canned
Hunt's stewed, 4 oz   30
Libby's whole, 1 cup   45
S & W whole, 1 cup   42
Stokely-Van Camp, whole   50
Townhouse, whole   50

Turnip Greens
Birds Eye 3.3 oz   20
Seabrook Farms, ½ cup   22
Stokely-Van Camp, ½ cup   22

Fruits and Vegetables, fresh, 1 cup unless noted

Asparagus	
cut spears	35
Bamboo shoots	
cuts	41
Bean Sprouts	37
Beans, green or snap	
cuts	34
Beans, wax or yellow	
cuts	30
Beet Greens	26
Cabbage, red or green, chopped	22
Cantelope, cubed	48
Casaba Melon, cubed	45
Cauliflower, flowerets	27
Swiss Chard, leaves only	32
Eggplant, diced	50
Radish, diced	20
Rhubarb, raw diced	20
Summer Squash, diced	35
Tomatos, sliced	40
Turnips, cubed	39

Fruit and Vegetable drinks, 6 oz

Cranberry	
Ocean Spray low calorie	35

Cranberry apple
Ocean Spray cranapple low calorie   30
Sauerkraut
Libby's   20
Tomato
Campbell's   35
Del Monte   35
Heinz   38
Hunt's   43
Libby's   39
S & W   22
Sacramento   35
Stokely-Van Camp   33
Townhouse   35
Welch's   38
Tomato cocktail
Ortega Snap-E-Tom   38
Vegetable cocktail
S & W   21
Townhouse   35
V-8   35

UNDER 20 CALORIES

Beverages

Note: virtually all sodas that are called *low-calorie*, *sugar-free* or *dietetic* contain 2 calories or less.

Bouillon, 1 cube

Beef
Herb-Ox	6
Maggi	6
Wyler's	7
Wyler's Instant	10

Chicken
Herb-Ox	6
Maggi	7
Wyler's	8
Wyler's Instant	6

Onion
Herb-Ox	10
Wyler's	6

Vegetable
Herb-Ox	6
Wyler's	6

Breath Mints, 1 piece

Certs clear	8
Certs pressed	6
Chewels	10
Clorets mints	6
Dentyne dynamints	2
Lifesavers	7
Trident mints	8

Broth, 1 packet

Herb-Ox

Beef	8
Chicken	12
Onion	14
Vegetable	12

Candy, Dietetic

Estee, 1 piece

chocolate covered raisins	6
gum drops	3
hard candies	12
mint candies	4

Cocktail Mix, non-alcoholic, 1 oz

Holland House Bloody Mary	6
Holland House Whiskey Sour	9

Coffee, 1 cup

ground	2
instant	4

Condiments, 1 Tbsp

A-1 sauce	12
Catsup	
Del Monte	15
Chili sauce	
Heinz	17
Horseradish	2
Mustard	
French's Brown	15
French's Yellow	16
Grey Poupon Dijon	15
Soy sauce	
La Choy	8
Taco sauce	
Old El Paso	4
Vinegar	1
Worcestershire	10

Cookies, 1 piece

Angel Puffs	
Stella D'Oro Dietetic	17
Arrowroot	
Sunshine	16
Royal Nuggets	
Stella D'Oro	1

Vanilla Snaps
 Nabisco   13
Vanilla Wafers
 Sunshine   15
 Nabisco   18
Zuzu Ginger Snaps
 Nabisco   16

Cough Drops   9

Crackers, 1 cracker

Cheez-It
 Sunshine   6
Cheeze
 Keebler   11
Flings Curls
 Nabisco   10
Matzos
 Manischewitz Tam Tams   14
Melba Toast
 Old London
  Garlic   9
  Onion   10
  Pumpernickel   17
  Rye   17
  Sesame   10
  Wheat   17
  White   17

Oyster
Keebler 3
Sunshine 3
Ritz
Nabisco 16
Saltines
Keebler Zesta 12
Nabisco Premium 12
Sunshine Krispy 11
Sociables
Nabisco 10
Triangle Thins
Nabisco 8
Wheat Thins
Nabisco 9

Creamers, Non-Dairy, 1 tsp

Coffee-Mate, Carnation, 1 pkt 11
Coffee-Tone 12
Cremora, Pet 11

Gelatin, mix, ½ cup

D-Zerta 8
Royal Sweet As You Please 6

Gravy, ¼ cup, mix

Au Jus
  Durkee 8
  French's 8
  McCormick 4
  Schilling 4
Brown
  Durkee 15
  Durkee with mushrooms 15
  Durkee with onions 17
  McCormick Lite 10
  Weight Watchers 8
    with mushrooms 12
    with onions 13
Chicken
  Durkee home style 18
  McCormick Lite 10
  Pillsbury home style 15
  Schilling Lite 10
  Weight Watchers 10
Mushroom
  McCormick 19
  Schilling 19
Pork
  Durkee 18
Mushroom Steak
  Dawn Fresh 4
Swiss Steak
  Durkee 11

Gum, 1 piece

Adams	9
Beeman	10
Beech-Nut	9
Beechies	6
Black Jack	9
Care Free	8
Chiclets	6
Clorets	6
Clove	5
Dentyne	5
Estee	3
Freshen-Up	9
Fruit Stripe	9
Orbit	8
Trident	5
Wrigley's	10

Jelly, 1 tsp

Ann Page, all flavors	18
Diet Delight Strawberry	18
Kraft, all flavors	16
S & W, all flavors	10
Smuckers Slenderella, all flavors	8

Oil

Pam Vegetable spray	7

Pickles

Capers, 1 Tbsp	
Crosse & Blackwell	6
Onions, cocktail, 1 Tbsp	
Crosse & Blackwell	1
Peppers, 1 oz	
Chile Green, *Ortega*	5
Hot Pickled, *Old El Paso*	9
Dill Pickles, spears, 1 piece	
Bond's	2
Del Monte	7
Heinz	7
Smucker's	8
Sour Pickles, 1 piece	
Del Monte	10

Salad dressings, 1 Tbsp

Blue Cheese	
Ann Page Low Calorie	18
Kraft Low Calorie	14

Tillie Lewis	12
Weight Watchers	10
Caesar	
Pfeiffer Low Calorie	10
French	
Pfeiffer Low Calorie	18
Weight Watchers	4
Tillie Lewis	12
Italian	
Ann Page Low Calorie	14
Kraft Low Calorie	6
Nu Made Low Calorie	16
Pfeiffer Low Calorie	10
Tillie Lewis	6
Weight Watchers	2
Red Wine	
Pfeiffer Low Calorie	10
Russian	
Pfeiffer Low Calorie	15
Tillie Lewis	12
Weight Watchers	12
Thousand Island	
Pfeiffer Low Calorie	15
Tillie Lewis	18
Weight Watchers	12

Sauces, 1 Tbsp

Barbecue
French's 14
Enchilada
Old El Paso hot 9
Old El Paso mild 10
Lemon-Butter
Weight Watchers 8

Sugar, 1 tsp 15

Pancake Syrup, 1 Tbsp

Cary's **Diet** 10
Diet Delight 15
S & W 12
Tillie Lewis 14

Tea, 1 cup 1

lemon-flavored
Nestea 2

Toppings, 1 Tbsp

No-Cal
  all flavors except chocolate and coffee   0
  No-Cal chocolate & coffee   6
whipped mix
  D-Zerta   8
  Dream Whip   10

Vegetables and Fruits, Fresh

Cabbage
  Chinese, cuts, 1 cup   11
  spoon (Bakchoy), cuts, 1 cup   11
Celery
  1 large outer stalk   7
  3 small inner stalks   9
Chicory greens
  cuts, 1 cup   11
  10 inner leaves   5
Endive, French or Belgian
  1 head, 5-7″   8
  10 small leaves   5
  chopped, 1 cup   14
Escarole, cuts, 1 cup   10
Mushrooms, chopped, 1 cup   20
Pepper, sweet, green, sliced, 1 cup   18

Pickles
 dill, 1 large   15
 sour, 1 large   14
Spinach, trimmed and chopped, 1 cup   14
Watercress, 1 cup   7

IMPROVE YOUR SELF WITH WARNER BOOKS

__HOW TO WEIGH LESS FOR THE REST OF YOUR LIFE
by Larry Adcock   *(L35-118, $2.75)*

This is more than a diet: it's a whole new approach to overweight. This is the one program that has worked even if you have been unsuccessful before. A step-by-step program, menu plans, tips for dealing with back-sliding, plus case histories.

__HOW TO LOOK TEN YEARS YOUNGER
by Adrien Arpel   *(L37-706, $9.95, U.S.A.)*
                      (L37-707, $11.95, Canada)

Adrien Arpel, president of her own multi-million dollar company, tells you how to give yourself a 10-years-younger image in just one day via her 5-step repackaging system; how to lift and trim your body in 10 minutes a day; how to follow the 24-hour emergency diet. She will also show you how to dress to hide body flaws as well as how to use makeup and win the big six skin battles to be wrinkle-free.

__LE GETTE'S CALORIE ENCYCLOPEDIA
by Bernard Le Gette   *(L90-919, $3.50)*

The most complete listing of calorie contents ever published. Includes: fast foods, brand-name foods, frozen foods, low-calorie foods, ethnic foods, and exotic foods.

WARNER BOOKS
P.O. Box 690
New York, N.Y. 10019

Please send me the books I have checked. I enclose a check or money order (not cash), plus 50¢ per order and 50¢ per copy to cover postage and handling.* (Allow 4 weeks for delivery.)

_____ Please send me your free mail order catalog. (If ordering only the catalog, include a large self-addressed, stamped envelope.)

Name _____

Address _____

City _____

State _____ Zip _____

*N.Y. State and California residents add applicable sales tax.   78